Waiting for the Dawn:
<u>*Mircea Eliade in Perspective*</u>

For Mircea and Christinel Eliade

As so often happens, scientists understand better than many "humanists" the meaning and function of artistic creativity. But we know now that artistic imagination has a mythological, i.e. *religious*, source. Consequently, a holistic system of knowledge—integrating the scientific, philosophic, religious, and artistic approaches and creations—might become again possible in the near future.

Of course, this is only a possibility, depending on what men will decide or will be able to do with their future. For the moment, we know—or we only feel, with "fear and trembling"—that we are entering into a new era.

> —Mircea Eliade, from
> speech entitled "Waiting for the Dawn"
> October 26, 1982, Boulder, Colorado

Waiting for the Dawn: Mircea Eliade in Perspective

David Carrasco and Jane Marie Law, editors

Foreword by Joseph Mitsuo Kitagawa
Photographs by Lawrence G. Desmond

University Press of Colorado

Photographs reproduced with permission of Lawrence G. Desmond.
Drawing of Mircea Eliade by Michael Wojczuk.

The University Press of Colorado is a cooperative publishing enterprise supported, in part, by Adams State College, Colorado State University, Fort Lewis College, Mesa State College, Metropolitan State College of Denver, University of Colorado, University of Northern Colorado, University of Southern Colorado, and Western State College.

Library of Congress Cataloging-in-Publication Data

Waiting for the dawn: Mircea Eliade in perspective / Davíd Carrasco and Jane Marie Law, editors; photographs by Lawrence G. Desmond; foreword by Joseph Mitsu Kitagawa. — Rev. ed.
    p. cm.
    Includes bibliographical references.
    ISBN 0-87081-239-4 (alk. paper)
    1. Eliade, Mircea, 1907– . 2. Religion. I. Eliade, Mircea, 1907– . II. Carrasco, David.
III. Law, Jane Marie.
BL43.E4W34 1991
291'.092 — dc20   91-34498
                                                              CIP

The paper used in this publication meets the minimum requirements of the American National Standard for Information Sciences—Permanence of Paper for Printed Library Materials. ANSI Z39.48–1984

∞

10 9 8 7 6 5 4 3 2

Contents

Illustrations

Acknowledgments

Many people played important roles in the conception and organization of this volume and the interdisciplinary faculty seminar from which it grew.

A special thanks goes to Frederick Denny who was chairman of the Department of Religious Studies during the year-long work on Mircea Eliade's writings. Fred's helpful ideas and leadership enabled the seminar to work smoothly. Other members of the department whose interest and ideas proved fruitful included Ira Chernus, Doris Havice, and Rodney L. Taylor. We are also grateful to William B. Taylor, a Latin American historian, for his thoughtful reflections on the intellectual character of the seminar and the book. Edward P. Nolan of Comparative Literature helped design the faculty seminar and proved to be an affirmative voice that supported and guided us. We also extend our appreciation to Robert Pois, an historian, for sharing his special enthusiasm for ideas, Eliade, and Eastern Europe.

A generous accolade is extended to Larry Senesh, co-president of the Academy of Independent Scholars, for his invitation to include this volume in the Academy's Retrospections Series. Larry's sense of humor plus the hospitality that he and Dorothy Senesh provided the Eliades during their visit to Boulder added a special warmth to the entire project. Others who helped make the Eliade visit a festive social and intellectual event were Ingrid and Mircea Fotino. Also a trusted friend, Douglas Fleckman, provided valuable encouragement and support throughout the seminar experience.

The meaning of the book has been significantly enhanced by Lawrence Desmond's superb photographic work. Thanks to Joan Gerthoeffer for typing the manuscript and to Irene Vasquez and Michael Wojczuk for helpful advice on the problems of design and fundraising.

Joseph M. Kitagawa, our teacher at the University of Chicago, assisted us in formulating the intellectual scope of the seminar and the content of the publication. We deeply value his continued support. The publication of this book was supported by a generous grant from the Committee on University Scholarly Publications at the University of Colorado.

Without the Committee's ideas and financial assistance the book could not have been published. Charles Long's lecture on Eliade's unique creativity formed part of the background from which the book emerged.

We are especially thankful to Sandy McCullough of Westview Press for her labor and thoughtfulness in getting the book published.

Most of all we are grateful for the presence and generosity of Mircea and Christinel Eliade.

D.C.
J.M.S.

Foreword

It is gratifying to know that *Waiting for the Dawn* is now available in paperback, for in my opinion this volume, despite its modest size, makes important contributions to unfolding the not-so-readily apparent spirit and intellectual contour of the eminent historian of religions and creative writer, Mircea Eliade.

Those of us who have closely followed Eliade's multidimensional career over the years have learned of the existence of subtle and intricate relationships between his life-long effort to "revise" (articulate and improve) various intellectual traditions handed down to him, and his valiant endeavor to "revision" the meaning of the religious universe and human orientation. Happily, *Waiting for the Dawn* vividly portrays Eliade's double orientation, in that, to him, the "revising" task in the scholarly sphere and his equally committed métier in "revisioning" the human mode of being are closely interrelated, indeed, inseparable.

Granted we learn much from some of the recent books and articles that extoll Eliade's prudent scholarly contributions to a wide range of subject matters, for example, Yoga, Shamanism, East European folklore, Australian religions, mysticism, and alchemy, to name just a few. Indeed, he had an insatiable curiosity and a firm determination to pursue a great variety of topics, events, and phenomena based on his conviction that the cosmos is a deposit of half-revealed and/or hidden meanings, and that it is our intellectual task to decipher those meanings by synthesizing the available knowledge of various disciplines and spheres.

It is worth knowing, however, that in many of his monographs Eliade repeatedly—and modestly—states that he is not a technical expert in those specialized disciplines and subject matters. He was of the persuasion that his efforts to decipher the implicit order of nature and the morphological arrangement of phenomena were not only essential to his vocation to "revise" and improve intellectual disciplines but were intrinsic to his endeavor to "revision" the total reality. This "revisioning" in turn enables our *mundus imaginalis* to catch a glimpse of the depth of the religious universe and to modify the quality of the human mode of being, which is otherwise boxed into the existential situation of temporality. Significantly, this motivation, vision, and dream of Eliade's runs through all his creative writings, too.

Recently, I was deeply touched by the tribute the freelance conductor Erich Leinsdorf paid to the composer Aaron Copland upon his death. He quoted a poignant Jewish prayer that states "man takes nothing with him, but his good works remain." I am equally convinced that the most precious legacy that Mircea Eliade has left behind is his two-pronged orientation of "revising" and "revisioning," as lucidly testified by *Waiting for the Dawn*.

Joseph Mitsuo Kitagawa

Prologue

PROMISE AND THE LABYRINTH

In his *Journal IV, 1979–1985* Mircea Eliade, who was in Paris at the time, wrote the following entry for September 11, 1982.

> Ruggiero Ruggieri writes me from Rome: I have been accorded the Premio Mediteraneo (two million lire) on the condition that I be present at Palermo on 20 and 21 October, because the prize is awarded only in person. I shall telephone tomorrow that "unfortunately" I cannot accept. On 2 October we leave for New York, on the seventh we'll be in Chicago, and on the twentieth (!) I must give the lecture long ago promised to Davíd Carrasco. An American scholar would not be impressed by a triple crossing of the Atlantic in three weeks, but in the state of fatigue which I find myself, for me it would be impossible.
>
> But refusing any "honors" in foreign countries and any dialogue or interview on radio or television (as I had to refuse the week-long *entretien* proposed by Chostel) limits my "publicity" to a minimum. I realize that my publishers aren't too happy about it.[1]

Like so many passages in Eliade's journals, this one is full of remarkable meanings, "discoveries . . . stray observations."[2] Seldom has a writer of journals been capable of combining such a rich array of place(s), memories, and time(s) with relationships between books, ideas, and people. These observations from Paris in 1982 are no exception, for we see Eliade choosing between a prize and a "promise," publicity and a lecture, transatlantic crossings and fatigue, Palermo and Colorado. For Eliade the question was simple: how to keep working? It is the "promise" Eliade made that organizes this new prologue to the paperback edition of *Waiting for the Dawn: Mircea Eliade in Perspective*, which contains, among other additions, his last novella, "In the Shadow of a Lily."

I want to say of Eliade what the Mexican writer José Emilio Pacheco said of Denis Diderot, that he is "unembraceable."[3] He had a career and an imagination you can't contain within your own reach or pen! He was a historian of religions, an editor of an encyclopedia, a novelist, an art critic, a teacher, philosopher, and journalist, and he did these things fully and with excellence. Something of his stature was evident to me from the beginning of my association with him. The map of that relationship is marked by the teachings of at least three other men, a Mexican, a black American, and an Englishman. Eliade was introduced to me by a Mexican, my writer/hero at the time, Octavio Paz, in his famous book *The Labyrinth of Solitude*. And Charles H. Long, a black American led me through the labyrinth of Eliade's thought. The finest written applications of Eliade's ideas were those of Paul Wheatley, whose writings on cities and symbols put me in a trance. While none of these men reduced Eliade to their historical condition, it was impressive that a Rumanian's imagination had qualities that illuminated both the Mexican and black experiences and struggles for creativity as well as the shape and power of the cities that were symbols. And in each case these writers were, in part, innovating Eliade's ideas. So, Eliade came to me not just through archaic myths and rituals, but through color, rebellion, politics, a sense of anguish, and a series of applications ranging from the structures of city-states to political and cultural movements. There was great promise in his writings. I am non-plused when some critics of Eliade restrict him through labels like "apolit-ical" and "ahistorical," as though he was not aware of the sources of historical change and political power.

When I first arrived at the University of Chicago's Divinity School in 1968, just after the Democratic National Convention had torn up Chicago's image as a city of law and order, Eliade's name was known to me only in a footnote, in Paz's "Dialectic of Solitude," the last chapter of *The Labyrinth of Solitude*. Strangely, I had carried Paz's book around in the trunk of my car for several years after my father gave it to me and only read it during my first quarter in the Divinity School. Unlike most students at the school, I had barely heard of Eliade until after I came to Chicago. It was Paz, in part, who brought Eliade to life when he wrote about the Mexican and wider human condition: "We have been expelled from the center of the world and are condemned to search for it through jungles and deserts or in the underground mazes of the labyrinth."[4]

The image of the labyrinth is used by many Latin American writers to show, among other things, the anguish and disorientation caused by the crushing experience of colonialism. Paz's study of the history and culture of Mexico, the psychological shape of the Mexican, the Mexican-American, masks, and nationalism, which made the author known to the wider world and was certainly one of the reasons for his Nobel Prize in Literature in 1990, is organized by the paradoxical, spatial image of the labyrinth, borrowed in part from Eliade. (See pages 208–212 in Paz.) In Paz's case the spatial image of the labyrinth, which both protects the center and is the complex path of *access* to the center, becomes the model for the interior world of Mexican politics, imagination, and psyche. So it was no surprise that years later, Eliade chose the labyrinth as the image to describe the wanderings, struggles, ideas, exile, and joys of his life in *Ordeal by Labyrinth: Conversations with Claude-Henri Rouquet.*

I cannot claim that Eliade took back from Paz part of what Paz took from him, but the associations are clearly there, and for a Chicano working to understand the history of religions, the political order, and nocturnal actions of the Mexican community in the city of Chicago in the early seventies, this image had special existential meanings for me as it has for many others. The promise I had felt in moving through Paz's labyrinth (guided secretly by Eliade) had been fulfilled somewhat in moving through Eliade's labyrinth (guided perhaps by Paz), while I was searching through my own labyrinths (guided by both). Since then I have discovered some of the uses, in Latin American literature, criticism, and archaeology, that are made of Eliade's ideas. And years later, when I named my son Octavio, I had many of these Paz/Eliade associations in mind.

If Eliade is "unembraceable," he can still be circumnavigated. This possibility came to me through one of his prize colleagues, Charles Long, who taught and retaught, figured, signified, and refigured Eliade for so many students in the Divinity School. It was clear to me that Long's understanding of Eliade's views were penetrating, on the mark, and sometimes uncovered hidden meanings in the master's work. Eliade himself made this claim about Long when he wrote of his own deep sense of loss when Long left Chicago in 1974 to assume a chair in the history of religions department at the University of North Carolina:

> He feels the need to know other university settings. . . . He undoubtedly has his reasons but I am crushed. Our friendship goes back to when I first arrived in the United States. Rare are those who know as well as he my views on the history of religions, and share them . . . he is in my opinion one of the rare people capable of conceiving a systematic and historical theology of archaic populations.[5]

Among Long's extraordinary capabilities was his genius for interpreting Eliade's archaic ontology to generations of students. He expressed regard for Eliade and displayed real insight as well as a series of innovations on Eliade's conceptions of space, initiation, liminality, the High God, millenarian consciousness, and the historical situation facing the student of the history of religions.[6]

An excellent example of scholarly collaboration came in Paul Wheatley's magisterial *The Pivot of the Four Quarters*, which included a comparative analysis of the pristine urban generation in Egypt, China, Mesopotamia, the Indus Valley, Nigeria, Peru, and Mesoamerica. Wheatley, through his capacity to read primary resources in these cultural areas plus his sensitivity to literary images, circumnavigated not only Eliade but parts of urban history as well. His application of Eliade's conceptions of archetypes and repetition in relation to spatial order was a special example of cumulative scholarship, that is, it used the work of our predecessors to raise new questions. In Wheatley's writings I discovered a disciplinary openness between urban geography, history of religions, archaeology, and ecology; a dialogue of genres.

These influences were in my mind when I approached Eliade in 1981 with the idea for a year-long seminar at the University of Colorado on the three genres of his career: history of religions, the novel, and autobiography. I explained that with the publication of the first volume of Eliade's *Autobiography*, the door to his personal journey was open for us to see influences and interactions in his three genres. I was particularly impressed by the possibility that aspects of the autobiography could be used as vehicles for seeing not only more Eliade "discoveries" but also his discoveries of "self." Even more important, it was time to have a *dialogue on the dialogue of genres* in his creativity.

Second, I explained that a "local knowledge" collaboration on his work would be valuable. Rather than bring a collection of Eliade "experts" to Colorado, I thought it crucial to tap the resources and talents of one particular university that would reflect within itself on the problems and significance of his contributions. This process of reflection and criticism would culminate, I hoped, in a week-long series of exchanges with Eliade in attendance; a dialogue of genres. He was delighted with the concept of the seminar and promised to come the following October.

The seminar and Eliade's visit were a success, and the result was the hardback *Waiting for the Dawn*, published locally by Westview Press. The story of the seminar is told in the original introduction, "Other Eliades," which appears later in this book.

As Eliade records in his *Mircea Eliade Journal IV, 1979–1985* he and Christinel returned to Boulder when *Waiting for the Dawn* was first published.[7] At that time, I asked Lawrence Desmond to take new photographs of the Eliades, and several have been included in the final section of this paperback edition. These are some of the last photos of him, taken less than a year before he died. The warm reception of the hardback plus the encouragement of Eliade's long-time friend and colleague, Joseph M. Kitagawa, who wrote the foreword for this volume, has led us to bring out this expanded version.

One of my attractions to Eliade was his literary creativity. While working in Religion and Literature at the Divinity School, I discovered some of Eliade's novellas and eventually *The Forbidden Forest*. I wanted to understand the ways in which he told stories and how those stories participated in the mythical and ritual worlds he had discovered, as well as how they reflected his personal life. While planning this paperback edition I had a hunch that one of Eliade's translators, Mac Linscott Ricketts, still had a few of Eliade's unpublished short stories. I wrote Ricketts about the project and presto! He generously offered Eliade's last known piece of fiction, "In the Shadow of a Lily," which had remained unpublished. In this remarkable, final, fragment of Eliade's literary imagination, which tells of trucks that disappear at midnight on a curve outside the city of Paris, we see him interweaving themes of exile, cargo cult, coincidence, paradise, riddles, and magic.

So, the promise that Eliade made and kept has ramified into the other meaning of promise. Eliade is one who not only made promises but *has promise*, has potential, a ground for expectation of excellence. The fulfillment of his promise resulted in a fine seminar, a special photographic record, and the earlier publication. And now the promise of his legacy has provided these renewed reflections on his work and, most significantly, the presentation to the English-speaking community of "In the Shadow of a Lily." With this publication I feel as though we have also kept a "promise" to him to represent his work fairly and in a renewed form. And as one promise may lead to another in the labyrinth of life, so this publication is done in the spirit of potential and openness reminiscent of what Carlos Fuentes, an enthusiastic admirer of Eliade, wrote about the novels of Diderot:

> The novel both reflects and creates an unfinished world made by men and women who are also unfinished. Neither the world nor its inhabitants have said their last word. The potential novel is thus the announcement and perhaps even the guaranty of a potential history. Of a potential life. We hope that we are part of an unfinished human presence expressing itself through narrative language.[8]

In closing I give one of Eliade's characters the last word about promise and the labyrinth. Eftimie states, ". . . signs are being made to us, but we pass them by without seeing them." The implication is: they continue to be made, and they wait to be seen.

David Carrasco
Boulder, Colorado

Notes

1. Mircea Eliade, *Mircea Eliade: Journal IV, 1979–1985* (Chicago: The University of Chicago Press, 1990), p. 67.

2. Mircea Eliade, *No Souvenirs: Journal, 1957–1969* (New York: Harper and Row, 1977), p. vii.

3. Carlos Fuentes, *Myself With Others* (New York: Farrar, Straus and Giroux, 1981), p. 72.

4. Octavio Paz, *The Labyrinth of Solitude* (New York: Grove Press, 1985), p. 209.

5. Mircea Eliade, *Mircea Eliade: Journal III, 1970–1978* (Chicago: University of

Chicago Press, 1989), p. 145.

6. See Long's recent work "Toward a Post Colonial Theory of Religion" where he establishes a new "arche" for the study of religion.

7. Mircea Eliade, *Mircea Eliade: Journal IV, 1979–1985* (Chicago: University of Chicago Press, 1990), p. 130-131.

8. Carlos Fuentes, op. cit, p. 88. It has become evident that many scholars have strong, invisible bonds with Eliade. Some bonds are appreciative, while others are hostile. The recent literature contains both insightful interpretations of his ideas and rebellious repudiations of his basic approach. Some scholars idealize Eliade, while others labor at "de-idealizing" or even destroying some of the grounds of his influence. Some who criticize yet openly benefit from his work express anger at both his influence and the undeveloped implications of some of his ideas. The important point is, perhaps, that his work set out a broad, rich, yet incomplete agenda that can be utilized in a number of hermeneutical and critical ways to achieve new understandings of homo religiosus.

DAVÍD CARRASCO
JANE MARIE LAW

—————— §§ ——————

Introduction: Other Eliades

On October 26, 1982, an extraordinary intellectual and social event took place at the University of Colorado at Boulder. The place was the Glenn Miller Ballroom in the University Memorial Center, scene of college dances, the famous "Trivia Bowl," public lectures, registration lines, and Buddhist assemblies. But this night's event transformed the room into yet another quality of space. Professor Mircea Eliade, the seventy-five-year-old Romanian-born novelist, and the world's leading historian of religions, delivered a brilliant lecture to a standing-room-only crowd of over 1,000 people from the Boulder academic community. The central ballroom, with its giant photograph of Glenn Miller with trombone on one wall and an imposing musical score of his song "Miller's Tune" on the other, had been set with five hundred chairs in expectation of a large turnout. But by half past seven, a half hour before the scheduled start of the lecture, all seats were taken. It was decided to accommodate the growing throng by opening the huge moveable doors on both sides of the ballroom, beyond which had been set up another five hundred chairs in anticipation of an overflow. Eliade, in a faculty seminar the next day, humorously referred to this opening of the giant doors as a "cosmogonic act." By eight o'clock, all seats were occupied—latecomers stood along the back walls.

The lecture, a section of which is included in this volume, demonstrated Eliade's vital capacity to reconsider the enterprise of the history of religions and think new thoughts about its role in the modern era. Concise in its points and amazing in its scope of data, the lecture included some of Eliade's most profound reflections on the human condition and man's quest to create and decipher meaning and value in his existence. It had, therefore, the appropriate title, "Waiting for the Dawn."

This small volume, which bears the same title as the lecture, is a product of an eight-month-long interdisciplinary faculty seminar dedicated to a critical study of Eliade's scholarly, literary, *and* autobiographical works. This seminar culminated in a week-long visit by Professor Eliade, accompanied by his charming wife Christinel, to the Boulder campus. During this visit, Eliade met twice with the seminar, which included scholars from the disciplines of Anthropology, Astrogeophysics, Comparative Literature, History, English, French, History, Mathematics, Molecular Biology, Philosophy, and Religious Studies.

The purpose of the entire seminar experience, organized by David Carrasco, an historian of religions at the University of Colorado, was to place Mircea Eliade's work in a new perspective. This perspective, represented in this volume, had three intended angles of vision. The first was suggested by the recent publication of Eliade's *Autobiography*, which had the appropriate symbolic subtitle, *Journey East, Journey West, Vol. I*. This publication clarified what had been previously indicated, namely that Eliade had produced not two but three types of writing including remarkable reflections on the labyrinthine quality of his professional and personal life. Our seminar was intended to view Eliade's contributions in terms of the threads of relationships between his academic, literary, and autobiographical works. In order to illustrate this wider perspective provided by Eliade himself, the editors of this volume, especially Jane Marie Swanberg, worked with Eliade in choosing eleven selections from his *oeuvre* that were either examined by the Eliade seminar or revealed special aspects of his work. The content of these selections are striking in their diversity: creative hermeneutics, literary imagination, autobiographical episodes, morphology and the sacred, excerpts from his novels, Freud, the terror of history, Charlie Chaplin, Romania, India, and nostalgia for initiation. These selections constitute the first section of this book entitled, "The Grand Oscillation: Selections from the *Oeuvre* of Mircea Eliade."

The second angle of vision emerged from a desire on the part of the editors to include in this volume a photographic record of Eliade working with scholars and students at this stage of his life. From having worked with Eliade in our student careers, we knew that even though he appeared as a luminous giant in the field of humanistic studies, he is comfortable and vital working with colleagues and students. Yet this important aspect of his career has hardly ever been mentioned. It seemed clear from reviewing other published works by or about Eliade, including the brilliant interviews in *Mircea Eliade: Ordeal by Labyrinth*, that very few thoughtful, artful photographs of Eliade have ever been published. To accomplish the process of recording Eliade on film, we invited a professional photographer, Lawrence Desmond, and a video tape technician, Douglas Fleckman, to record a number of events during Professor Eliade's visit to Boulder. A special selection of Desmond's photographs appear throughout this volume.

The third approach in our attempt at a new perspective was decidedly interdisciplinary. In the planning of the seminar, we felt that in order to arrive at a shared vision of the scope of Eliade's *oeuvre*, it was necessary to assemble a lively group of scholars from a wide number of fields in the academy. Our idea was to draw upon the insights of not only historians of religions but also scholars who came to Eliade's work from other intellectual circles and disciplines. Participants in the seminar included Mike Bell from English; Davíd Carrasco, Ira Chernus, Frederick Denny, Doris Havice, and Rodney Taylor from Religious Studies; Ingrid Fotino from Mathematics; Mircea Fotino from Molecular Biology; Reginald Ray from Naropa Institute; Kim Malville from Astrogeophysics; Dennis McGilvrey from Anthropology; Jacques Barchilon from French; Edward Nolan from Comparative Literature; Phyllis Kenevan from Philosophy; and Jane Marie Swanberg, a Ph.D. student in the history of religions from the University of Chicago, on leave during that term. While we asked only three of these participants to produce essays for the book, the contributions of each were essential to the dynamic, interdisciplinary endeavor that the seminar became.[1] The reader will gain insight into the seminar's activities in Robert Pois's article, "Sacred Space, Historicity, and Mircea Eliade," which opens the second section of this book entitled, "Encounter and Reflections: Essays by Seminar Participants." As these essays indicate, the seminar was an encounter not only with the works of Mircea Eliade, but with the man himself. Seminar participants, in dialogue with Professor Eliade on different aspects of his work, came to new understandings of not only his work but their own as well.

Prior to Eliade's visit, the seminar participants read, discussed, and prepared oral responses to numerous readings from his works including *Myth of the Eternal Return*, "Cultural Fashions and the History of Religions," *Yoga: Immortality and Freedom; Two Tales of the Occult; Patterns in Comparative Religions; Myths, Dreams and Mysteries; The Forbidden Forest;* and *Mircea Eliade, Autobiography: Journey East, Journey West, Vol. I, 1907–1937.* When Eliade arrived in Boulder, the group was prepared to discuss specific aspects of his work as well as raise questions concerning the general significance of his interpretations. It was within this intellectual context that we heard "Waiting for the Dawn." Because of Eliade's previous commitment to publish a version of the Boulder lecture in the forthcoming *The History of Religions: Retrospect and Prospect*, edited by Joseph M. Kitagawa, we have included only a section of the lecture in this volume.

This volume is obviously an homage to Eliade as well as a critical review of certain aspects of his work. As the recent awards, festschrifts, and celebrations of Eliade demonstrate, he does not need an homage. But one of the underlying goals of this volume is to expand our understanding, in a modest fashion, as well as our appreciation of this remarkable man. This is no simple task. In the last twenty years, a debate has brewed concerning the value, significance, and scope of Eliade's contributions to Western scholarship and literature. As Edward P. Nolan points out in his essay "The Forbidden Forest: Eliade as Artist and Shaman," Eliade's approach has resulted in incredible acclaim and sometimes "less lovely . . . even vicious" reactions by members of the scholarly community. From T. J. Altizer's claim that Eliade is "the greatest living interpreter of the whole world of primitive and archaic religions" to Jonathan Z. Smith's clever comparison of Eliade to the Giant on whose shoulder we all stand "without the attendant claim of having seen farther," to Bob Pois's comparison of the changes brought about in his own thought during the "Eliade experience" with the subtleties of the first atomic reaction at the University of Chicago, to Edmund Leach's distorted assessment that Eliade's works are sermons by a man on a ladder, the responses to his accomplishments have been intense and large. The most substantial English language assessments of Eliade's work appear in two fine collections of essays, namely, *Myths and Symbols: Studies in Honor of Mircea Eliade*, edited by Joseph Kitagawa and Charles H. Long (1969) and the more recent *Imagination and Meaning: The Scholarly and Literary Worlds of Mircea Eliade*, edited by Norman Girardot and Mac Linscott Ricketts (1982). The former volume contains articles about myths and symbols in world religions and assessments of some of Eliade's literary works by distinguished scholars and friends. The range and strength of many of these essays will probably never be surpassed. The latter work contains essays by students and specialists of Eliade's work as well as important fragments of his Romanian writings appearing for the first time in English. Both of these outstanding collections limit their perspective of Eliade to what Girardot calls "the twin scholarly and literary passions of his career." The present work claims that a third passion has found its way into Eliade's career, namely the autobiographical journey of orienting the self. As Rodney Taylor demonstrates in his essay "Mircea Eliade: The Self and the Journey," Eliade's previous reflections on his life, such as appears in *No Souvenirs*, do not represent the same kind of personal, literary creativity as that found so distinctly in the *Autobiography*. For this reason alone, the present volume, which owes much to these two previous publications, can be thought of as an attempt, in part, to see "another" Eliade. This does not mean that we re-read his academic and literary works in the new light provided by the *Autobiography*. That strategy was considered and voted down. It means that we attempted to perceive the tissues of insight and understanding that linked the academic, literary, and auto-biographical dimensions of Eliade together.

This approach is reflected in not only the selections from Eliade's work but also in the essays that complete the volume. Robert Pois, a professor of History at the University of Colorado narrates his own intellectual resistance, fascination, and growth during the seminar. This process, which he labels the "Eliade experience" led him, while reflecting on his journey to Eastern Europe, the historian Frederick Meinecke, historicism, and Eliade's lecture to the discovery of a "sacred space" occupied by historians while writing history. Pois's "voice" and insights constitute a special contribution to our understanding of Eliade's and Pois's approaches to the category of history. Edward P. Nolan of the Department of Comparative Literature courageously took the job of locating the place of Eliade's magnum opus novel *The Forbidden Forest* within the mainstream of the Western literary tradition. In an insightful twist, Nolan illuminates Eliade's literary vision and strategy by comparing it to not only the "modern connoisseurs of chaos," Proust, Kafka and Dostoevsky, which has been done elsewhere, but also to special moments in the works of Ovid and Virgil. Nolan's insights into the artistic strategies in *The Forbidden Forest* break new ground in understanding Eliade the novelist. In his view, Eliade is a "master of a kind of positive stoicism." The volume concludes with Rodney Taylor's measured treat-ment of the *Autobiography*. An historian of religions with special expertise in the genre of religious autobiography, Taylor's work illuminates how Eliade's autobiographical search for self-orientation, self-discovery, and self-evaluation constitutes a distinct form of religious creativity as well as a genuine probing of the self. Through sensitively focusing on special moments in Eliade's memories of his adolescence in Romania, his early compositions, his journey to India, his powerful relationship with his guru Dasgupta, Taylor provides us with an illuminating view of Eliade's life and creativity, which has not appeared in print before.

In a recent discussion on the future of the History of Religions discipline, the distinguished scholar, Ninian Smart referred to an earlier assessment he made of Eliade's place in scholarship.

I have recently written a paper, called "Beyond Eliade" which uses tran-scendence in the best possible way, that is, you affirm the reality of that which you transcend. You give it high marks but say that maybe there is something beyond it.[2]

Our claim is that an authentic usage of Eliade as a foundation for going beyond him must be based, in part, on an accurate understanding of not only the quality of his brilliance but also the massive and multi-dimensional contributions he has made and is making. These are important aspects of what Smart must mean by "the reality of that which you transcend." It appears that a number of scholars are making claims of having gone beyond Eliade when in fact they have not yet arrived at the place he so generously occupies. It is appropriate, in this sense, that we give Eliade the last word of this introduction. We include here a passage he wrote on the hermeneutics of understanding the universe of religion through a comparison with the universe of aesthetics. What he writes about coming to grips with the contributions of Balzac can be said to be appropriate strategies for understanding his own contributions as well.

> If the work of Balzac can hardly be understood without a knowledge of nineteenth-century French society and history (in the broadest meaning of the term—political, economic, social, cultural and religious history) it is nonetheless true that the *Comedie Humaine* cannot be reduced to a historical document pure and simple. It is the work of an exceptional individual, and it is for this reason that the life and psychology of Balzac must be known. But the working out of this gigantic *oeuvre* must be studied in itself, as the artist's struggle with his raw material, as the creative spirit's victory over the immediate data of experience. A whole labor of exegesis remains to be performed after the historian of literature has finished his task, and here lies the role of the literary critic. . . . But can a literary work be said to be finally "explicated" when the aesthetician has said his last word? There is always a secret message in the work of great writers. . . .[3]

Notes

1. A number of excellent oral presentations gave life to the seminar meetings in the months prior to Eliade's visit. Ira Chernus from Religious Studies gave an outstanding presentation on the thematic relationship between parts of *Yoga: Immortality and Freedom* and *Two Tales of the Occult*. Kim Malville from Astro-geophysics drew a number of fascinating parallels between Eliade's work on cosmogonic myths and recent theories of the creation of the universe postulated by astronomers. Mircea and Ingrid Fotino, Eliade's countrymen, provided valuable historical reflections and anecdotes about the Romanian culture, Eliade's reputation, and his contributions as viewed in Eastern Europe. Fred Denny, chairman of Religious Studies that year, presented an appreciative critique of *Patterns in Comparative Religions* that included a series of questions on the relation of Islamic materials to Eliade's model.

2. Ninian Smart, "History of Religions," *Religious Studies Review,* vol. 5, no. 3, 1979.

3. Mircea Eliade, "A New Humanism," *The Quest* (Chicago: University of Chicago Press, 1969), p. 5.

——§§——

PART ONE

The Grand Oscillation: Selections from the Oeuvre of Mircea Eliade

─────────────$\mathcal{S}\mathcal{C}$─────────────

Waiting for the Dawn

The selections that follow are taken from Professor Eliade's lecture "Waiting for the Dawn," delivered at the University of Colorado on October 26, 1982.

Discovering the East

It has been remarked that one paradox characteristic of the post-war period is the coexistence of a tragic, neurotic pessimism with a robust, candid optimism. A great number of scientists, sociologists, and economists draw increasing attention to the imminent catastrophes which menace our world—not only our Western type of culture and socio-political institutions but mankind in general and even life on this planet. On the contrary, other authors, less numerous but equally energetic, exalt the great scientific discoveries and the fantastic technological conquests accomplished, or underway, in recent decades. . . . Although they approach their subjects from opposing positions, these thinkers illustrate different aspects of the same cultural process. . . .

Tragically pessimistic or utterly optimistic, both trends of thought proclaim the imminent end of our world. Both predictions—Apocalypse or Golden Age—have a religious structure, in the sense that they partake of a religious symbolism. Of course, the representatives of these two opposite trends are not aware of the religious implications of their despair or of their hopes. What is significant is that all believe in the inevitability and the imminence of *our* world's end.

I do not have the competence to discuss such different and contradictory predictions. Instead, I will examine a series of recent signs indicating,

───────────

0

These selections from Professor Eliade's lecture "Waiting for the Dawn," which was originally presented on October 26, 1982, at the University of Colorado, are reprinted here with the permission of the author.

more or less clearly, that historically, culturally, and spiritually we are entering, or ready to enter, a new era. As I have repeated on many occasions, the most significant event of our century is not the "proletarian revolution," but the active presence in history of Asia and of the "primitive world"—the Third World. In the perspective of cultural history—the only one which interests us here—the discovery of Asiatic and archaic spiritual traditions already bears significant consequences and will effect considerably more in the future. The mystique of the proletarian liberation is of a Judeo-Christian origin and interests primarily the Western world. The discovery (or re-discovery) of the value and significance of non-Western spiritualities represents *a cultural innovation*, for it launches a dialogue and an interrelationship with *the others*, that is, the representatives of Asiatic and archaic traditions.

I shall not insist on the first consequence of such encounters with oriental spiritualities. One could cite the wide interest, both in Europe and in the United States, in Yoga and Hinduism, in Zen and different Buddhist schools of thought and meditation techniques, in Tantra, in *The Tibetan Book of the Dead*, in the *I Ching* and Taoism, etc. Certainly, in many cases these reflect a kind of fad; the understanding of the *authentic* meanings and messages of such traditions is sometimes inadequate and purely emotional or, even worse, erroneous and counterfeit. Moreover, we must keep in mind the risk of pseudomorphoses, of cultural alienation and spiritual sterility, for such hazards confront any encounter with new, foreign, or unknown spiritual worlds. Nevertheless, the number of Americans and Europeans who seriously study such texts is increasing steadily. Furthermore, even a superficial infatuation with fashionable "oriental" vocabulary, ideas, and meditation techniques constitutes a positive cultural phenomenon: it helps to "deprovincialize" the Western traditions.

The creative results of encounters with oriental spirituality are, for the moment, rather modest. But if we recall the impact of Japanese painting and African art on European artists during the second part of the nineteenth and early twentieth century, there can be little doubt as to the positive results of contemporary encounters with oriental traditions. This time, however, we will not witness a repetition of the nineteenth-century failure to assimilate the "Oriental Renaissance" prophesied by Schopenhauer. Although he read the Upanishads only in a very approximate Latin translation (the *Oupnekhat*, 1801–1802, by Anquetil-Duperron), Schopenhauer was so deeply impressed that he compared the revelation of "Indian wisdom" to discovery of the authentic Greek heritage which stimulated the Italian Renaissance. During the fifteenth century the newly discovered works were passionately read by philosophers, theologians, and artists alike, whereas, unfortunately the Sanskrit and Pali texts attracted almost exclusively the interest of philologists, linguists, and historians. We must also keep in mind that at that time, a number of specific Indian and Indo-Tibetan philosophical systems and ascetic techniques—for instance, Yoga, Tantra, Mahayana—were either neglected or misunderstood.

In the last thirty years the situation radically changed. On the one hand, many inaccessible oriental works were translated and competently interpreted; on the other hand, such works are read by an increasing number of artists, philosophers, and scientists. The impact of Zen and Tantra on many young American writers and artists is too well known to insist upon. It is reported that Robert L. Oppenheimer began to study Sanskrit after reading some classical Upanishads; he admitted that their cosmology was the only one which made sense to a contemporary physicist. It is also reported that, in his old age, Heidegger read *Isa Upanishad* for the first time and remarked that he would like to have written in such a "style."

I do not need to recall the passionate interest of C. G. Jung in the *I Ching*. For the moment I would like to point out the title of the recent best-seller: *The Tao of Physics* (Berkeley: 1975) by the high-energy physicist, Fritjov Capra. One could say that the "wisdom of the East" begins to impress itself on the representatives of Western genius. But the phenomenon is even more complex: It involves the whole contemporary *Zeitgeist* which makes possible such *rapprochement* between the old Chinese conception of the universe and the most recent scientific discoveries. The Romanian-born French philosopher Stephane Lupasco has elaborated a new logical system of metaphysics. Marc Beigbeder, his most gifted interpreter, compares Lupasco's system to the dynamic complementarity of yin and yang and claims that the yin-yang complementarity is the only existing model which approached Lupasco's. As an old friend and admirer of Stephane Lupasco, I may add that he did not know anything about Taoism; most probably, he discovered the existence of Tao, yin, and yang by reading Beigbeder's book on his philosophy.

Shamanism, Hallucinogens, Initiation

Significantly, at least in the United States, the most *creative* encounter was with archaic—as a matter of fact, prehistoric—spiritual values. For the first time in his (not so long) history, modern man became contemporary with his paleolithic and neolithic relatives, that is to say, he understood and reiterated their mode of being in the world. Indeed, the recent discovery of shamanism by artists and the youth-culture constitutes, in itself, a fascinating episode in the history of ideas. Only

thirty years ago shamanism had a rather limited interest even for specialists—i.e., anthropologists and historians of religions. When, in the forties, I began studying Siberian and Central Asian shamanism, only two monographs on the topic existed; today there is a considerable bibliography in most of the Western European languages. A generation ago shamanism was considered to be either a psychopathic phenomenon, a primitive healing practice, or an archaic type of black magic, but contemporary scholarship has convincingly demonstrated the complexity, the rigor, and the rich spiritual meaning of shamanistic initiations and practices.

The "existential" interest of American youth in shamanism and shamanistic techniques was abundantly illustrated by the reaction to Carlos Castenada's books: *The Teachings of Don Juan* (1968), *A Separate Reality* (1971), *Journey to Ixtlan* (1972), *Tales of Power* (1974), and *The Second Ring of Power* (1977). These books not only became best-sellers, but also created a "para-shamanistic underground movement," especially in California. In another connection, professors of theatre like Theodore Kirby, rightly detected in shamanism one of the origins of drama. Moreover, shamanistic techniques are employed in experimental performances of the so-called "Alternative Theatre." Along the same line, a handsomely published volume—*Stones, Bones and Skin: Ritual and Shamanistic Art* (Toronto: 1977)—contains a number of articles on some contemporary artistic creations produced by utilizing shamanistic techniques. One may add other examples of poets and musicians who relate their works to shamanistic mythologies and methods.

Probably such interest was incited in great part by the fascination of the youth-culture with hallucinogens, especially LSD. I will not discuss here this serious and intricate problem. What strikes an historian of religions is the fact that the "trips" obtained through hallucinogens have an "ecstatic" structure and are acknowledged as such by some users of LSD. Evidently, without a spiritual preparation, the "trips" cannot become a "mystic experience." But it is important to notice that a part of contemporary youth tries to reactualize an archaic, prehistoric technique, even if the results are, medically speaking, more or less disastrous.

In traditional societies, the future shaman *begins* by being ill. The syndrome of his mystical vocation is characterized by strange and even pathological behaviour: he easily loses consciousness, takes refuge in the forests, throws himself into water or fire, wounds himself with knives. But this is a *"maladie initiatique."* The future shaman's psychopathological crises do not belong to ordinary symptomatology; they are of an *initiatory pattern and meaning.* His physical pains and psychomental disorders represent a series of initiatory ordeals; his symbolic death is always followed by a "resurrection" or a "rebirth," manifested by his radical cure and by the appearance of a new, more structured, stronger personality.

Such an "existential" interest in shamanism and the awareness of the psycho-mental risks involved in hallucinogens, may have another consequence in the near future: helping contemporary Western man undergo sickness (both physiological and psycho-mental) as a series of *initiatory ordeals*. In other words, any affliction would be considered and "realized" as an "occasion" for the integration of personality and spiritual transformation: that is to say, the contemporary equivalent of traditional initiation.

Literary Imagination and Religious Structure

This essay presents Mircea Eliade's conception of the alternating modes of the creative human spirit, the "diurnal," rational mode of scholarship and the "nocturnal," mythological mode of imagination and fantasy.

In one of his lesser known books, *The Philosopher and Theology,* Etienne Gilson wrote the following: "There are times when a person must have the courage to provide the critics with an easy method of getting rid of him." Well, I suppose I must have this courage because, instead of discussing literary imagination and religious structures *in general,* I will speak also of my own literary activity and its relation to my work as a historian of religions.

Now, in the Anglo-American academic milieu, not so long ago, it was rather unwise for a scholar to be also known as a writer of fiction. (Poetry was usually accepted; somehow, it was not taken seriously.) One of the luminaries of neo-positivism, Professor Ayer—the only living philosopher to be called a "second Hobbes"—thought that he could not better discredit Jean-Paul Sartre and the existentialist philosophers than by entitling his devasting critique of them in the journal *Mind:* "Philosophers-Novelists."

As you know, Bertrand Russell became famous for his inexhaustible and imaginative audacity, not only in philosophy and mathematics, but also in ethics, in politics, and in his understanding of personal freedom

"Literary Imagination and Religious Structure" is the text of a lecture presented at the University of Chicago in 1978. The entire text is reprinted here with the permission of *Criterion Magazine,* vol. 17, no. 2 (Summer 1978):30–34, (Chicago: University of Chicago Divinity School).

(in his *Autobiography*, he did not hesitate to speak of his many extra-marital love affairs). Nevertheless, Bertrand Russell did not publish, during his lifetime and under his name, the short stories which he so much enjoyed writing. He did not care about losing his respectability, but he did not want to endanger his reputation as a "serious" thinker. His literary pieces were brought out in a handsome volume only a few years after his death.

There are, of course, exceptions and Giorgio Santayana is one of them. He *did* have the courage to sign and print his novel, *The Last Puritan*. But one wonders if he did not do it on purpose, just to annoy his colleagues. Oliver, the hero of *The Last Puritan*, says he is going to become a professor because he does not think he is "fit for anything else." And another character remarks: "People must *teach themselves* or remain ignorant—and the latter was what the majority preferred." Santayana considered the profession of teaching almost exclusively as a means of subsistence—and especially as a means of being able to go to Europe every year. But, as I said, Santayana was an exception. During one of his classes, he suddenly looked through the window, then addressed the students: "I have a date with spring," he told them, and he left. And he never came back. . . .

As you know, things have changed in the last thirty years, at least in Europe. Jean-Paul Sartre brought out a volume of short stories, *Le Mur*, and his novel, *La Nausée*, a few years before *L'Etre et le Néant*, and almost at the same time, he became extraordinarily popular as a playwright. Likewise, Gabriel Marcel published philosophical books and many plays, and Merleau-Ponty was writing a novel in the very year of his death. Moreover, he told his friends that by working on this novel he was able to formulate his philosophical insights better and more adequately than in his theoretical books.

I must add, however, that, born in Romania near the turn of the century, I belong to a cultural tradition that does not accept the idea of the incompatibility between scientific investigation and artistic, especially literary, activity. As a matter of fact, some of the most original Romanian scholars have also been successful writers, and the greatest of Romanian poets—Mihail Eminescu—was also a philosopher and one of the most learned men of his time. Long before the new fashion of the French artist-philosopher, it was not uncommon for a Romanian scholar to be acclaimed as a poet, a novelist, or a playwright.

In my case, I soon discovered that such a double vocation was part and parcel of my destiny. While yet a very young man, I realized that no matter how captivated I might be by oriental studies and the history of religions, I would never be able to give up literature. For me, the writing of fiction—short stories, novellas, novels—was more than a "violon d'Ingres"; it was the only means I had of preserving my mental health, of avoiding neurosis. I shall never forget my first year at the University of Calcutta; from January until the beginning of the summer of 1929, I devoted myself exclusively to the study of Sanskrit. I worked some fourteen to fifteen hours a day and did not allow myself to read in any language except Sanskrit, not even, after midnight, a page from the *Divina Commedia* or the Bible. And suddenly, at the beginning of summer, I sensed I had to escape from the prison in which I had locked myself. I needed *freedom*—that freedom which the writer knows only in the act of literary creation. For several days I tried, in vain, to resist the temptation to put aside the Sanskrit grammar, the dictionaries of Apte and Monier-Williams and Aniruddha's *Saṃkhya-sutṛavrui*, and write the novel that was obsessing me. In the end, I *had* to write it; I wrote *Isabel and the Devil's Sea* in a matter of a few weeks, and only after that did I regain my desire to work. I returned then with enthusiasm to the study of Sanskrit grammar and Saṃkhya philosophy.

Twenty years later, on June 21, 1949, in Paris, when I was drafting a chapter of *Le Chamanisme*, I felt all of a sudden the same temptation to begin a novel. This time too I tried to resist. I said to myself, quite correctly, that it would be of no use to write a literary work in Romanian—a book which could not appear in Romania and for which I should have to find a translator and above all a publisher; since, at that time, I was completely unknown as a writer in France, it would have been difficult to persuade an editor to publish such a novel. In my *Journal* for that summer, I noted several desperate efforts that I made to ward off the temptation to begin *The Forbidden Forest*. For some time, I hoped I could continue working on *Le Chamanisme* during the daytime while devoting a part of the night to the novel. But soon I realized that I could not live at the same time in two worlds—that of scientific investigation and that of literary imagination—and, at the beginning of July, I interrupted *Le Chamanisme* in order to be able to concentrate on the novel. It was to take five years for me to finish it, because I did not find enough time, or the right "inspiration," except for two or three months a year.

I said to myself that my spiritual equilibrium—the condition which is indispensible for any creativity—was assured by this oscillation between research of a scientific nature and literary imagination. Like many others, I live alternately in a diurnal mode of the spirit and in a nocturnal one. I know, of course, that these two categories of spiritual activity are interdependent and express a profound unity, because they have to do with the same "subject"—*man*—or, more precisely, with the mode of existence in the world specific to man, and his decision to assume this mode of existence. I know likewise from my own experience that some of my literary creations contributed to a more profound understanding of certain religious structures, and that, sometimes, without my being conscious of the fact at the moment of writing fiction, the literary imagination utilized materials or meanings I had studied as a historian of religions.

So, it was with great joy that I read this observation by J. Bronowski: "The step by which a new axiom is adduced cannot itself be mechanized. It is a free play of the mind, an invention outside the logical processes. This is the central act of imagination in science, and it is, in all respects, like any similar act in literature." This means, however, that literature is, or can be, in its own way, an instrument of knowledge. Just as a new axiom reveals a previously unknown structure of the real (that is, it *founds* a new world), so also any creation of the literary imagination reveals a new universe on meanings and values. Obviously, these new meanings and values endorse one or more of the infinite possibilities open to one for *being* in the world, that is for *existing*. And literature constitutes an instrument of knowledge because the literary imagination reveals unknown dimensions or aspects of the human condition.

In epic literature (novella, story, novel), literary imagination utilizes narrative scenarios. They may be as different as the scenarios attested in *The Quest of the Grail, War and Peace, Carmen, A la recherche du temps perdu,* or *Ulysses.* But in one way or another, all these creations of epic literature *narrate* something—more or less dramatically, more or less profoundly. Of course, the *forms* in which the narratives are presented— from *The Golden Ass* to *Père Goriot*, from Dostoevsky to *Absalom, Absalom!* and *Dr. Faustus*—can appear antiquated; in any event, few contemporary writers would dare to repeat epic formulas used by their great predecessors. But this does not mean, as has been believed, the "death of the novel"; it means simply that many of the classical forms of the "roman-roman"—the "novel as narrative"—are superannuated; that consequently we must invent new narrative forms.

This is not the place to enter into the recent fervent discussion about the decisive importance—in fact, the tyranny—accorded to language, an importance which, according to some, would justify not only "la nouvelle vague" of the novel, but also the other contemporary attempts to write unintelligible (or at any rate unreadable) prose. I wish only to recall that discoveries made recently in linguistics can help revive lyrical poetry, but they do not annul the importance and necessity of narrative literature. It would require too much time for me to analyze the function and significance of this literature. The specific mode of existence of man implies the necessity of his learning what happens, and above all what *can* happen, in the world around him and in his own interior world.

That it constitutes a structure of the human condition is shown, among other things, by the *existential necessity* of listening to stories and fairy tales even in the most tragic of circumstances. In a book about Soviet concentration camps in Siberia, *Le Septième Ciel,* J. Biemel declares that all internees, almost a hundred in number, living in his dormitory, succeeded in surviving (while in other dormitories ten or twelve died each week) because they listened every night to an old woman telling fairy tales. So greatly did they feel the need for stories that every one of them renounced a part of his daily food ration to allow the old woman not to work during the day, so she could conserve her strength for her inexhaustible story-telling.

Quite as revealing in my view are the experiments carried out in several American universities in connection with the physiology and psychology of sleep.

One of the four phases of sleep is called REM (Rapid Eye Movement); it is the only phase during which the sleeping person dreams. The following experiments were done: Volunteers were prevented from staying in the REM phase, but were permitted to sleep. In other words, they could sleep, but it wasn't possible for them to dream. Consequence: the following night, the persons deprived of REM tried to dream as much as possible, and if they were again prevented from doing so, they proved to be nervous, irritable, and melancholy during the day. Finally, when their sleep was no longer bothered, they gave themselves over to veritable "orgies of Rapid Eye Movement sleep," as if they were avid to recover everything they had lost during the preceding nights.[1]

The meaning of these experiments, it seems to me, is clear: they confirm the organic need of man to *dream*—in other words, the need for "mythology." At the oneiric level, "mythology" means above all *narration,* because it consists in the envisioning of a sequence of epic or dramatic episodes. Thus man, whether in a waking state or dreaming (the diurnal or the nocturnal modes of the mind), needs to witness adventures and happenings of all sorts, or to listen to them being narrated, or to read them. Obviously, the possibilities of narrative are inexhaustible because the adventures of the characters can be varied infinitely. Indeed, characters and events can be manifest on all levels of the imagination, thereby making possible reflections of the most "concrete" reality as well as the most abstract fantasy.

A closer analysis of this organic need for narrative would bring to light a dimension peculiar to the human condition. It could be said that man is par excellence an "historic being," not necessarily in the sense of the different historicistic philosophers from Hegel to Croce and Heidegger, but more particularly in the sense that man—any man—is continually fascinated by the chronicling of the world, that is, by what happens in his world or in his own soul. He longs to find out how life is conceived, how destiny is manifest—in a word, in what circumstances the impossible becomes possible, and what are the limits of the possible. On the other hand, he is happy whenever, in this endless "history" (events, adventures, meetings, and confrontations with real or imaginary personages, etc.) he recognizes familiar scenes, personages, and destinies known from his own oneiric and imaginary experiences or learned from others.

For me, a historian of religions and an orientalist, the writing of fiction became a fascinating experience in method. Indeed, in the same way as the writer of fiction, the historian of religions is confronted with different structures of sacred and mythical space, different qualities of time, and more specifically by a considerable number of strange, unfamiliar, and enigmatic worlds of meaning. Each literary piece creates its own proper universe, and the creation of such imaginary universes through literary means can be compared with mythical processes. For any myth relates a story of a creation, tells how something came into being—the world, life, or animals, man and social institutions. In this sense, one can speak of a certain continuity between myth and literary fiction, since the one as well as the other recounts the creation (or the "revelation") of a new universe. Of course, myth has also an exemplary value in traditional societies, and this is no longer true for literary works. One must keep in mind, however, that a literary creation can likewise reveal unexpected and forgotten meanings even to a contemporary, sophisticated reader.

In sum, as I have said, literary creation can be considered an *instrument of knowledge:* knowledge, of course, of other worlds parallel to the everyday world. There is a structural analogy between the universe of meaning revealed by religious phenomena and the significant messages expressed in literary works. Any religious phenomenon is a hierophany, i.e., a manifestation of the sacred, a dialectical process that transforms a profane object or act into something that is sacred, i.e., significant, precious, and paradigmatic. In other words, through a hierophany, the sacred is all at once revealed and disguised in the profane. (It is disguised for everyone else outside that particular religious community.) Likewise, in the case of literary works, meaningful and exemplary human values are disguised in concrete, historical, and thus fragmentary characters and episodes. Investigating and understanding the universal and exemplary significations of literary creations is tantamount to recovering the meaning of religious phenomena.

This is why a writer or a literary critic is usually better prepared to understand the documents investigated by the historian of religions than, say, a sociologist or an anthropologist. Writers and literary critics *believe in the reality and the significance of artistic creations*, i.e., they are convinced by their own labors of the objectivity and the intellectual value of the *mundus imaginalis*, of the imaginary universe created or discovered by any significant author. As you know, a number of literary critics, in Europe as well as in the United States, interpret literary creations in a perspective borrowed from the historian of religions. Myth, ritual, initiation, cultural heroes, ritual death, regeneration, rebirth, etc., belong now to the basic terminology of literary exegisis. To quote one single example: there are a considerable number of books and articles analyzing the initiation scenarios camouflaged in poems, short stories, and novels. Such scenarios have been identified not only in Jules Verne's novels or in *Moby Dick*, but also in Thoreau's *Walden*, in the novels of Cooper and Henry James, in Twain's *Huckleberry Finn*, and in Faulkner's "The Bear." Quite recently, Professor Vierne, of the University of Aix-en-Provence, published a book entitled *Ritual, Initiation and the Novel*. And in his *Radical Innocence* (1966), Professor Ihab Hassan consecrates an entire chapter to the "dialectics of initiation," using as examples the writings of Sherwood Anderson, F. Scott Fitzgerald, Wolfe, and Faulkner.

More than ten years ago, while investigating precisely this interest of the literary critics in the initiation patterns camouflaged in novels, short stories, and poems, I suggested that such research may also be significant for an understanding of modern Western man. And I would like to conclude with what I wrote then:

The desire to decipher initiatory patterns in literature, plastic arts, and cinema denotes not only a reevaluation of initiation as a process of spiritual regeneration and transformation, but also a certain nostalgia for an equivalent experience. In the Western world, initiation in the traditional and strict sense of the term has disappeared long ago. But initiatory symbols and scenarios survive on the unconscious level, especially in dreams and imaginary universes. It is significant that these survivals are studied today with an interest difficult to imagine fifty or sixty years ago. Freud has shown that certain existential tendencies and decisions are not conscious. Consequently, the strong attraction toward literary and artistic works with an initiatory structure is highly revealing. Marxism and depth psychology have illustrated the efficacy of the so-called demystification when one wants to discover the *true*—or the *original*— significance of a behavior, an action, or a cultural creation. In our case, we have to attempt a demystification in reverse; that is to say, we have to "demystify" the apparently profane worlds and languages of literature, plastic arts, and cinema in order to disclose their "sacred" elements, although it is, of course, an ignored, disguised, or degraded "sacred." In a desacralized world such as ours, the "sacred" is present and active chiefly in the imaginary universes. But imaginary experiences are part of the total human being, no less important than his diurnal experiences. This means that the nostalgia for initiatory trials and scenarios, nostalgia deciphered in so many literary and plastic works, reveals modern man's longing for a total and definitive renewal, for a *renovatio* capable of radically changing his existence.

Notes

1. Mircea Eliade, *No Souvenirs*, Fred H. Johnson, Jr., trans. (New York: Harper & Row, 1977), 279–280.

––––––––––§§––––––––––

Sambo

This passage about the room Sambo *is from Professor Eliade's magnum opus novel* The Forbidden Forest.

He sat on the edge of the bed and looked at them both intently. "Please don't interrupt me. Now that Anisie has become a literary character, I too can reveal the secrets of my childhood. I'll tell you the story of the room *Sambo*. . . . I was about five or six years old," he began, his voice hushed, "and I found myself with my family at Movila. We were living in a kind of villa-hotel that had two floors and about fifteen or twenty rooms. In the dining room we sat next to a group of very mysterious young people. They seemed mysterious to me because although they spoke Romanian, I couldn't understand very well what they were saying. From time to time one of them pronounced a foreign word, without significance for me, and then they all began to exclaim, to become excited, and to raise their voices. Their mysteriousness fascinated me. And one day I turned my head suddenly toward their table at a moment when the discussion had become exceptionally animated. I heard one of them—the one who seemed oldest because he had a mustache—say something, and I saw him raise his arm toward the ceiling, apparently to indicate a direction. I heard him utter in a solemn voice the word 'Sambo.' Suddenly they all fell silent. They bent their heads and looked down at their plates. Then one after another they repeated: 'Sambo!' 'Sambo!' . . . At that instant I felt a thrill I had never known before. I felt that I'd penetrated a great and terrible secret. All the mysteries of the men at the nearby table were concentrated in

From *The Forbidden Forest*, (Notre Dame: Notre Dame University Press, 1981), pp. 74–78. This selection is reprinted here with permission of Notre Dame University Press and the author. The translation into English is by Mac Linscott Ricketts and Mary Park Stevenson.

25

those two syllables, '*Sambo!*' Through a providential circumstance I had turned my head at the exact moment when the man with the mustache pointed out the place where their secret, *Sambo*, was found. It was above us, somewhere overhead on the second floor. And of course I set out that very afternoon to discover it.

"We children slept with our nurse in a separate room next to that of our parents. I pretended to go to sleep and when I sensed that the *doica* was dozing I went out. I ran down the hall as fast as I could and climbed up to the second floor, my heart pounding. I didn't know where to go but I felt my heart beating harder and harder. I closed my eyes in fright and began to walk softly on the carpet toward the end of the hall. I don't know how far I went, but I found myself in front of a door, and just at that moment I knew that there was where *Sambo* was! I wondered later how I found the courage to put my hand to the latch and go in. I was trembling all over and if I had heard a loud noise at that moment, or a scream, I probably would have fainted. Nevertheless, I took hold of the latch and went in. . . .

"I can see it now. The shades were drawn and in the room there was a mysterious half-light, a coolness of a totally different nature from the coolness of other rooms I had been in before. I don't know why, but it seemed to me that everything there was suspended in a green light—perhaps because the curtains were green. The room was full of all sorts of furniture and chests and baskets of papers and magazines and old newspapers. But to me it seemed that it was green. And just then, at that moment I understood what *Sambo* was. I understood that here on earth, near at hand and yet invisible, inaccessible to the uninitiated, a privileged space exists, a place like a paradise, one you could never forget in your whole life if you once had the good fortune to know it. Because in *Sambo* I felt I was no longer living as I had lived before. I lived differently in a continuous inexpressible happiness. I don't know the source of this nameless bliss.

"Later, when I would think about *Sambo* I was sure that God had been waiting for me there and had taken me in his arms as soon as I stepped across the threshold. I have never, at any place or any time, felt such happiness; not in any church or art museum—nowhere—ever. Each time I went, I must have stayed there for hours, because whenever I returned to my family I found them upset and worried, occasionally even furious. 'Where have you been?' they demanded. 'We've been looking for you for three hours!' 'I was playing,' I lied, and no amount of threatening, no punishment, frightened me. I accepted everything with a smile, comforted by the thought that I would be able to return to *Sambo*. . . . Once I went there with several pieces of candy in my pocket. Without realizing it I put one in my mouth and began to suck it. Impossible! It had no flavor. I couldn't suck it. My mouth was dry. I couldn't move my tongue. I couldn't do anything in *Sambo*. I wasn't hungry, I wasn't thirsty, I wasn't sleepy. I lived, purely and simply, in paradise. . . .

"On the evening of the day when I had gone there with the candy I noticed that the men at the table beside me looked at me furtively and talked in whispers among themselves, pointing at me. Of course I realized then that they knew about my crime. They knew that I'd entered *Sambo* with candy in my pocket and had even tried to eat a piece. I believe the sense of shame and the fear that I had been discovered were the cause of the indigestion I had. For two days I lay ill. The nurse told me later that I talked in my sleep, that I was delirious although I didn't have very much fever. I had an idea of what I might have talked about but I didn't think I'd betrayed myself. The rest of my family didn't know about *Sambo*. They hadn't turned their heads in time to see the direction indicated by the man with the mustache. . . . I waited impatiently to be allowed to get out of bed.

"On the third day as we were returning from the beach I managed to slip away from their watchful eyes and ran to the second floor. But I couldn't get in. *Sambo* was locked. I was crushed. I stayed there for a long while, trying the latch from time to time. In vain. *Sambo* remained locked. I prayed in my mind as I had been taught to pray. I recited all the prayers I knew, to God, to the Holy Mother, to Jesus Christ, and to my Guardian Angel, but *Sambo* remained locked. I prayed in my mind to the man with the mustache. I prayed to everyone at his table, those powerful men who knew unintelligible words, who were initiated into mysteries—and then trembling I put my hand on the latch. In vain. The door still didn't open. I had been forbidden to enter. *Sambo* had become inaccessible to me.

"I came back the next day and the day after. I came back every afternoon, as long as our holiday at Movila lasted. I came in vain. It had been forbidden me to enter *Sambo*. I was aware of this besides when I spied on my neighbors at the next table. They didn't look at me anymore. They stopped raising their voices, and always spoke in whispers with their heads bowed. I found out the reason for this from the *doica*. The man with the mustache had been drowned on the beach at Tuzla. They didn't bring him back to Movila. He was shipped directly to Constanta. I didn't tell them anything, but I knew why he had drowned. . . .'"

"In other words, you had a guilt-complex," interrupted Biris.

"No, I don't think it was that. I didn't have any feeling of guilt, but it seemed to me I knew something. I had participated in a mystery along with all the others at the neighboring table. And this mystery involved, among other things, a death. . . . That's all. . . ." He stopped, exhausted, and lit another cigarette.

"But, actually, what was *Sambo?*" Ileana asked. "Whatever could this word *Sambo* have meant?"

Stefan smiled. "I don't know that myself, but it's not very important. Later when I was in the *liceu* I wondered if perhaps those young men had been discussing literature, and if all those foreign words that had thrilled me weren't titles of books and names of authors. Maybe the man with the mustache had uttered the word *Salammbo* emphatically, and had raised his arm high at the same time. I might have thought that he had said *Sambo* and that he was pointing to the second floor. . . . But even if this were so my experience of the mystery remains no less valid. Actually, perhaps all those literary discussions had only one purpose—of which the men who took part in them were unaware— the purpose of revealing to me the experience of the mystery. I don't want to go into the details now. . . . I've told you the story of the room *Sambo* so that you'd understand why I can't offer you anything in this secret room, why I can't even give you a sweet. Here in the secret room I cannot eat."

"If I understand you rightly," commented Biris, "this room is a replica of the room *Sambo*. You're trying now as an adult to find again that ineffable experience of childhood. . . . A psychoanalyst might call it a case of infantile regression."

"No, I don't think you're right. This secret room has another story. It's too long to tell you now. Besides, I don't know if I could tell it successfully. But I'm sure it's a very different matter. I recall a thought which obsessed me when I was very young: what could I do to acquire a different identity? That is, to be a different man from the one I knew I had begun to be; a man endowed with certain intellectual tendencies, conditioned by certain social and moral complexes, with certain tastes and certain habitual reactions. What should I do, I asked myself, to be able to live in a way that was differnt from the way I felt myself obliged to live, obliged not only by family or society, but even by myself, by my own past, by my own *history*, as Biris would say? To give you an example: I like certain authors and consequently I felt obliged to like them all the time. I had convinced myself that I like them, and I felt I'd be contradicting myself if I should declare some day that I didn't like them anymore. On the day I did that I'd have the feeling that I had repudiated myself, that I was inconsistent, so to speak, that I had no continuity of ideas. Well, now, in this secret room I'm free to contradict myself, free to believe what I like, even if those beliefs and opinions are ephemeral. . . ."

"It is, you might say, an extra-historical and atemporal room," said Biris, beginning to laugh cheerfully.

"It is that indeed," Stefan continued fervently, "but it's also something more. I won't be able to tell you everything because I don't know how to express such obscure thoughts. . . ."

"Better show us your paintings. Maybe we'll understand what it's all about when we've seen them."

Gravely Stefan looked first at one and then the other. He ran his hand across his face and smiled. "This is the very thing that's so hard to explain," he began after a long silence, "because these paintings I want to show you conceal a great secret, and if I don't reveal it to you beforehand, I doubt you'll be able to see them."

"I don't quite understand what you mean," said Biris, "but all the same I think it might be better for you to begin by showing us the paintings."

Stefan was silent again, embarrassed.

"You told me you'd show me the car," Ileana said suddenly. "And if you want to know the truth that's what I came for—to see the car. If it had been a matter of any other kind of pictures perhaps I'd have refused. I could have come to see them some other time. But, I said to myself, maybe that midnight car can only be seen at night. That's why I came. . . ."

Stefan continued to look at them in deep silence, almost frowning.

"You told me, 'Anch'io sono pittore!' " Ileana insisted.

"And I am!" Stefan exclaimed all at once. "In my way, I also am a painter. But it's a very special picture. In order to understand it properly . . ."

At that moment they heard a voice from the room next door, a powerful voice with a provincial accent: "Show them the painting, *domnule*, and cut the gab! Show them right now, get it over with! It's midnight. Let us sleep!"

Stefan stood petrified in the middle of the room. Amused, Ileana smiled and motioned toward the next room. "Answer him something," she whispered quickly. "Tell him something to quiet him."

Stefan approached her on tiptoe. "Do you think he heard it too?" he asked in an excited whisper. "Do you think he could have heard the story about the room *Sambo?*"

"No, he couldn't have," Ileana soothed him, still whispering. "I know when he came in. I heard him. It was just a few minutes ago."

"You're sure he didn't hear?" Stefan asked again, greatly disturbed. Ileana nodded.

"Show us now, before he goes to sleep," whispered Biris, approaching Stefan.

"Impossible," Stefan said very softly. "I have to explain."

"Hang the explanations!" Biris interrupted impatiently, "It's late. At least show us one canvas. . . ."

"Just show us the car," whispered Ileana.

Stefan passed his hand over his face again, shaking with excitement. "There's only one canvas," he said at length. "There's just one and the same canvas for all my pictures. That's why I said I have to explain it to you, so you'll know how to look at it. Ileana's car, for instance, is the last picture I painted, but I painted it on the same canvas with all the other pictures. And as you can see, it's necessary I explain to you how to look at it. Otherwise you won't be able to recognize it."

"What does that matter?" exclaimed Biris in exasperation. "Show us the canvas—we'll figure it out for ourselves. We'll find the car, don't you worry. . . . !"

"But if I tell you it's one and the same canvas?" Stefan raised his voice.

"Then why did you call me?" Ileana asked. "You told me you'd show me the car."

"I'm going to show it to you." Stefan insisted, "but only after I explain what I painted before I painted the car."

"What a stubborn man he is!" came the voice from the next room again. "God really made a stubborn one this time!" and he pounded furiously on the wall several times with his fist. "Will you show it to them, *domnule,* or shall I go call the porter?"

"I can't show it to them," cried Stefan, "because they don't know how to look at it!"

—————— §%· ——————

From Silkworms to Alchemy

This selection from Autobiography, Volume I: Journey East, Journey West, *1907–1937 recounts Eliade's experience of writing his first published article at the age of fourteen.*

I still remember very well my first published article: "The Enemy of the Silkworm," which appeared in *Ziarul Ştiinţelor Populare* (The Newspaper of Popular Sciences) in the spring of 1921. I had entered the fourth year of lycée and was living alone in my little attic room, because Nicu had gone to attend military school at Tîrgu-Mureş. I had spent the summer with the whole family at the half-rebuilt "Villa Cornelia" at Tekirghiol. I had been bored, having come with few books; and after finishing them I sought desperately for something to read—anything. In a closet I found Vasile Conta's *Complete Works*, and I stubbornly read through them all, without always understanding them. The rest of the time I collected plants, snails, and insects. I began writing a study about the fauna and flora of Tekirghiol, which I later reworked and published in the winter of 1922 in *Ziarul Ştiinţelor Populare*.

I don't know what made me choose as the subject of my very first article the "enemy of the silkworm." The subject did not particularly attract me, and at that time I knew enough about entomology to have

Professor Eliade began writing his memoirs in the early 1960s at the age of 65. Volume 1 of his *Autobiography, Journey East, Journey West 1907–1937*, recounts his life up until the age of 30, after his return from India. Volume 2, which he began in the late 1970s, will soon be released. Volume 1 was originally published by the Romanian Emigre Press Destin in Madrid. This translation, by Professor Mac Linscott Ricketts, appeared in English in 1981 (San Francisco: Harper & Row, 1981). The selections from the *Autobiography*, which appear in this volume "From Silkworms to Alchemy," "Vocation and Destiny: Savant not Saint," and "The Criterion Group: From Freud to Charlie Chaplin" are reprinted with the permission of Harper & Row Publishers and the author.

written something more significant. Probably I told myself that, since the subject had its practical aspect, it would have a greater chance of being published. It was signed "Eliade Gh. Mircea." When I saw my name in print—in the abstract and again at the end of the article—my heart began to pound. All the way home from the stand where I had bought the paper, it seemed to me that everyone was looking at me. In triumph I showed it to my parents. Mother pretended not to have time to read it. Probably she wanted to savor it at leisure, the way I know she read some of my articles later. But Father put on his glasses and read it on the spot (it was no longer than a column). "It doesn't have much value," he said. "It's a patchwork."

So it was, indeed. I tried to explain to him that in this article I was not doing "science" but "popularization," something just as important and necessary as original research. However, I don't think I convinced him.

A few months later *Ziarul Ştiinţelor Populare* announced a contest for lycée students. With great excitement I read the rules. It was exactly what I had dreamed of doing; a scientific topic to be treated in a literary fashion. I composed a brief fantasy entitled "How I Found the Philosopher's Stone." It began something like this: I am in my laboratory, and for some reason or other I have fallen asleep (but of course the reader didn't know this, because I did not tell him). There appears a strange character who talks to me about the Philosopher's Stone and assures me that it is no legend, that the stone can be obtained if you know a certain formula. He tells me about a lot of operations performed by famous alchemists, which he has witnessed, and he proposes that we reconstruct the experiment together. He has not convinced me, but I agree. The stranger mixes different substances in a crucible, places it over the fire, then sprinkles some powder on it and exclaims: "Watch closely now! Watch!" In truth, the substances in the crucible are transformed into gold before my very eyes! In my excitement I make an abrupt gesture, knocking the crucible to the floor. At that instant I awake and find myself alone in the laboratory. But for a moment the dream seems to have been a reality: a crucible really is lying on the floor, and beside it is a piece of gold. Only after I pick it up do I realize that it is pyrite or "fool's gold."

I never reread that story, but when I thought about it, decades later, I realized that it was not without significance. When I wrote it I was enthusiastic about chemistry and knew almost nothing about alchemy. At that time I loved matter, I believed in it; I knew the immediate utility of different substances, but I was also fascinated by the mystery of chemical structures, the countless combinations possible among molecules. Not until several years later did I discover, in the library of the

King Carol I Foundation, *Collection des anciens alchimistes grecs* by Marcellin Berthelot. Soon after that I felt strongly attracted to alchemy, and since then I have never lost interest in the subject. In 1924–1925 I published my first articles about Alexandrian and Medieval alchemy in *Ziarul Ştiinţelor Populare*. While studying at the university, I wrote to Prophulla Chandra Ray, and he sent me from Calcutta his two volumes on Indian alchemy. When I was in India (1928–1931), I collected a rich body of material that I used in the series of articles first published in *Vremea* and republished as a monograph, *Alchimia Asiatică* (Asian Alchemy), in 1935. Then followed *Cosmologie şi Alchimie Babiloniană* (Babylonian Cosmology and Alchemy) in 1937, *Metallurgy, Magic, and Alchemy* in 1938, and *The Forge and the Crucible* (*Forgerons et Alchimistes*) in 1956—this last book resuming and developing the themes of the earlier works. At that time I knew nothing about Jung's researches. I tried to demonstrate, nevertheless, that alchemy was not a rudimentary chemistry, a "pre-chemistry," but a spiritual technique, seeking something entirely different from the conquest of matter; seeking, at bottom, the transmutation of man: his "salvation" or liberation.

What I wouldn't give to be able to read that story again now, to find out what that mysterious character revealed to me, what alchemistic operations he had witnessed! I had found, *in dreams*, the Philosopher's Stone. Only decades later was I to understand, after having read Jung, the meaning of that oneiric symbolism.

———————§✢———————

A New Humanism

"A New Humanism," from Eliade's book of essays The Quest: History and Meaning in Religion, *explores the role of the enterprise of history of religions in bringing about an integrated humanistic endeavor in the academies.*

Despite the manuals, periodicals, and bibliographies today available to scholars, it is progressively more difficult to keep up with the advances being made in all areas of the history of religions.[1] Hence it is progressively more difficult to become a historian of religions. A scholar regretfully finds himself becoming a specialist in *one* religion or even in a particular period or a single aspect of that religion.

This situation has induced us to bring out a new periodical. Our purpose is not simply to make one more review available to scholars (though the lack of a periodical of this nature in the United States would be reason enough for our venture) but more especially to provide an aid to orientation in a field that is constantly widening and to stimulate exchanges of views among specialists who, as a rule, do not follow the progress made in other disciplines. Such an orientation and exchange of views will, we hope, be made possible by summaries of the most recent advances achieved concerning certain key problems in the history of religions, by methodological discussions, and by attempts to improve the hermeneutics of religious data.

————————————

"A New Humanism," which appears in Mircea Eliade's work *The Quest: History and Meaning in Religion* (Chicago: University of Chicago Press, 1969), pp. 1–11, is a revised and expanded version of his original article entitled "History of Religions and a New Humanism," which was first published by the journal *History of Religions*, 1 (1961):1–8. It is reprinted here in its longer form with permission of the University of Chicago Press and the author.

Hermeneutics is of preponderant interest to us because, inevitably, it is the least-developed aspect of our discipline. Preoccupied, and indeed often completely taken up, by their admittedly urgent and indispensable work of collecting, publishing, and analyzing religious data, scholars have sometimes neglected to study their meaning. Now, these data represent the expression of various religious experiences; in the last analysis they represent positions and situations assumed by men in the course of history. Like it or not, the scholar has not finished his work when he has reconstructed the history of a religious form or brought out its sociological, economic, or political contexts. In addition, he must understand its meaning—that is, identify and elucidate the situations and positions that have induced or made possible its appearance or its triumph at a particular historical moment.

It is solely insofar as it will perform this task—particularly by making the meanings of religious documents intelligible to the mind of modern man—that the science of religions will fulfill its true cultural function. For whatever its role has been in the past, the comparative study of religions is destined to assume a cultural role of the first importance in the near future. As we have said on several occasions, our historical moment forces us into confrontations that could not even have been imagined fifty years ago. On the one hand, the peoples of Asia have recently reentered history; on the other, the so-called primitive peoples are preparing to make their appearance on the horizon of greater history (that is, they are seeking to become *active subjects* of history instead of its *passive objects*, as they have been hitherto). But if the peoples of the West are no longer the only ones to "make" history, their spiritual and cultural values will no longer enjoy the privileged place, to say nothing of the unquestioned authority, that they enjoyed some generations ago. These values are now being analyzed, compared, and judged by non-Westerners. On their side, Westerners are being increasingly led to study, reflect on, and understand the spiritualities of Asia and the archaic world. These discoveries and contacts must be extended through dialogues. But to be genuine and fruitful, a dialogue cannot be limited to empirical and utilitarian language. A true dialogue must deal with the central values in the cultures of the participants. Now, to understand these values rightly, it is necessary to know their religious sources. For, as we know, non-European cultures, both oriental and primitive, are still nourished by a rich religious soil.

This is why we believe that the history of religions is destined to play an important role in contemporary cultural life. This is not only because an understanding of exotic and archaic religions will significantly assist in a cultural dialogue with the representatives of such religions. It is more especially because, by attempting to understand the existential situations expressed by the documents he is studying, the historian of religions will inevitably attain to a deeper knowledge of man. It is on the basis of such a knowledge that a new humanism, on a world-wide scale, could develop. We may even ask if the history of religions cannot make a contribution of prime importance to its formation. For on the one hand, the historical and comparative study of religions embraces all the cultural forms so far known, both the ethnological cultures and those that have played a major role in history; on the other hand, by studying the religious expressions of a culture, the scholar approaches it from within, and not merely in its sociological, economic, and political contexts. In the last analysis, the historian of religions is destined to elucidate a large number of situations unfamiliar to the man of the West. It is through an understanding of such unfamiliar, "exotic" situations that cultural provincialism is transcended.

But more is involved than a widening of the horizon, a quantitative, static increase in our "knowledge of man." It is the meeting with the "others"—with human beings belonging to various types of archaic and exotic societies—that is culturally stimulating and fertile. It is the personal experience of this unique hermeneutics that is creative. It is not beyond possibility that the discoveries and "encounters" made possible by the progress of the history of religions may have repercussions comparable to those of certain famous discoveries in the past of Western culture. We have in mind the discovery of the exotic and primitive arts, which revivified modern Western aesthetics. We have in mind especially the discovery of the unconscious by psychoanalysis, which opened new perspectives for our understanding of man. In both cases alike, there was a meeting with the "foreign," the unknown, with what cannot be reduced to familiar categories—in short, with the "wholly other."[2] Certainly this contact with the "other" is not without its dangers. The initial resistance to the modern artistic movements and to depth psychology is a case in point. For, after all, recognizing the existence of "others" inevitably brings with it the relativization, or even the destruction, of the official cultural world. The Western aesthetic universe has not been the same since the acceptance and assimilation of the artistic creations of cubism and surrealism. The "world" in which preanalytic man lived became obsolete after Freud's discoveries. But these "destructions" opened new vistas to Western creative genius.

All this cannot but suggest the limitless possibilities open to historians of religions, the "encounters" to which they expose themselves in order to understand human situations different from those with which they are familiar. It is hard to believe that experiences as "foreign" as those of a paleolithic hunter or a Buddhist monk will have no effect whatever on modern cultural life. Obviously such "encounters" will become culturally creative only when the scholar has passed beyond the stage of pure erudition—in other words, when, after having collected, described, and classified his documents, he has also made an effort to understand them *on their own plane of reference*. This implies no depreciation of erudition. But, after all, erudition by itself cannot accomplish the whole task of the historian of religions, just as a knowledge of thirteenth-century Italian and of the Florentine culture of the period, the study of medieval theology and philosophy, and familiarity with Dante's life do not suffice to reveal the artistic value of the *Divina Commedia*. We almost hesitate to repeat such truisms. Yet it can never be said often enough that the task of the historian of religions is not completed when he has succeeded in reconstructing the chronological sequence of a religion or has brought out its social, economic, and political contexts. Like every human phenomenon, the religious phenomenon is extremely complex. To grasp all its valences and all its meanings, it must be approached from several points of view.

It is regrettable that historians of religions have not yet sufficiently profited from the experience of their colleagues who are historians of literature or literary critics. The progress made in these disciplines would have enabled them to avoid unfortunate misunderstandings. It is agreed today that there is continuity and solidarity between the work of the literary historian, the literary sociologist, the critic, and the aesthetician. To give but one example: If the work of Balzac can hardly be understood without a knowledge of nineteenth-century French society and history (in the broadest meaning of the term—political, economic, social, cultural, and religious history), it is nonetheless true that the *Comédie humaine* cannot be reduced to a historical document pure and simple. It is the work of an exceptional individual, and it is for this reason that the life and psychology of Balzac must be known. But the working-out of this gigantic *œuvre* must be studied in itself as the artist's struggle with his raw material, as the creative spirit's victory over the immediate data of experience. A whole labor of exegesis remains to be performed after the historian of literature has finished his task, and here lies the role of the literary critic. It is he who deals with the work as an autonomous universe with its own laws and structure. And at least in the case of poets, even the literary critic's work does not exhaust the subject, for it is the task of the specialist in stylistics and the aesthetician to discover and explain the values of poetic universes. But can a literary work be said to be finally "explicated" when the aesthetician has said his last word? There is always a secret message in the work of great writers, and it is on the plane of philosophy that it is most likely to be grasped.

We hope we may be forgiven for these few remarks on the hermeneutics of literary works. They are certainly incomplete,[3] but they will, we believe, suffice to show that those who study literary works are thoroughly aware of their complexity and, with few exceptions, do not attempt to "explicate" them by reducing them to one or another origin—infantile trauma, glandular accident, or economic, social, or political situations, etc. It serves a purpose to have cited the unique situation of artistic creations. For, from a certain point of view, the aesthetic universe can be compared with the universe of religion. In both cases, we have to do at once with *individual experiences* (aesthetic experience of the poet and his reader, on the one hand, religious experience, on the other) and with *transpersonal realities* (a work of art in a museum, a poem, a symphony; a Divine Figure, a rite, a myth, etc.). Certainly it is possible to go on forever discussing what meaning one may be inclined to attribute to these artistic and religious *realities*. But one thing at least seems obvious: Works of art, like "religious data," have a mode of being that is peculiar to themselves; they *exist on their own plane of reference*, in their particular universe. The fact that this universe is not the physical universe of immediate experience does not imply their nonreality. This problem has been sufficiently discussed to permit us to dispense with reopening it here. We will add but one observation: A work of art reveals its meaning only insofar as it is regarded as an autonomous creation; that is, insofar as we accept its mode of being—*that of an artistic creation*—and do not reduce it to one of its constituent elements (in the case of a poem, sound, vocabulary, linguistic structure, etc.) or to one of its subsequent uses (a poem which carries a political message or which can serve as a document for sociology, ethnography, etc.).

In the same way, it seems to us that a religious datum reveals its deeper meaning when it is considered on its plane of reference, and not when it is reduced to one of its secondary aspects or its contexts. To give but one example: Few religious phenomena are more directly and more obviously connected with sociopolitical circumstances than the modern messianic and millenarian movements among colonial peoples (cargo-cults, etc.). Yet identifying and analyzing the conditions that prepared and made possible such messianic movements form only a part of the work of the historian of religions. For these movements are equally creations of the human spirit, in the sense that they have become what they are—*religious movements*, and not merely gestures of protest and revolt—through a creative act of the spirit. In short, a religious phenomenon such as primitive messianism must be studied just as the *Divina Commedia* is studied, that is, by using all the possible tools of scholarship (and not, to return to what we said above in connection with Dante, merely his vocabulary or his syntax, or simply his theological and political ideas, etc.). For, if the history of religions is destined to further the rise of a new humanism, it is incumbent on the historian of religions to bring out the autonomous value—the value as *spiritual creation*—of all these primitive religious movements. To reduce them to sociopolitical contexts is, in the last analysis, to admit that they are not sufficiently "elevated," sufficiently "noble," to be treated as creations of human genius like the *Divina Commedia* or the *Fioretti* of St. Francis.[4] We may expect that sometime in the near future the intelligentsia of the former colonial peoples will regard many social scientists as camouflaged apologists of Western culture. Because these scientists insist so persistently on the sociopolitical origin and character of the "primitive" messianic movements, they may be suspected of a Western superiority complex, namely, the conviction that such religious movements cannot rise to the same level of "freedom from sociopolitical conjuncture" as, for instance, a Gioachino da Fiore or St. Francis.

This does not mean, of course, that a religious phenomenon can be understood outside of its "history," that is, outside of its cultural and socioeconomic contexts. There is no such thing as a "pure" religious datum, outside of history, for there is no such thing as a human datum that is not at the same time a historical datum. Every religious experience is expressed and transmitted in a particular historical context. But admitting the historicity of religious experiences does not imply that they are reducible to nonreligious forms of behavior. Stating that a religious datum is always a historical datum does not mean that it is reducible to a nonreligious history—for example, to an economic, social, or political history. We must never lose sight of one of the fundamental principles of modern science: *the scale creates the phenomenon.* As we have recalled elsewhere,[5] Henri Poincaré asked, not without irony, "Would a naturalist who had never studied the elephant except through the microscope consider that he had an adequate knowledge of the creature?" The microscope reveals the structure and mechanism of cells, which structure and mechanism are exactly the same in all multicellular organisms. The elephant is certainly a multicellular organism, but is that all that it is? On the microscopic scale, we might hesitate to answer. On the scale of human vision, which at least has the advantage of presenting the elephant as a zoological phenomenon, there can be no doubt about the reply.

We have no intention of developing a methodology of the science of religions here. The problem is far too complex to be treated in a few pages.[6] But we think it useful to repeat that the *homo religiosus* represents the "total man"; hence, the science of religions must become a total discipline in the sense that it must use, integrate, and articulate the results obtained by the various methods of approaching a religious phenomenon. It is not enough to grasp the meaning of a religious phenomenon in a certain culture and, consequently, to decipher its "message" (for every religious phenomenon constitutes a "cipher"); it is also necessary to study and understand its "history," that is, to unravel its changes and modifications and, ultimately, to elucidate its contribution to the entire culture. In the past few years a number of scholars have felt the need to transcend the alternative *religious phenomenology* or *history of religions*[7] and to reach a broader perspective in which these two intellectual operations can be applied together. It is toward the integral conception of the science of religions that the efforts of scholars seem to be orienting themselves today. To be sure, these two approaches correspond in some degree to different philosophical temperaments. And it would be naive to suppose that the tension between those who try to understand the *essence* and the *structures* and those whose only concern is the *history* of religious phenomena will one day be completely done away with. But such a tension is creative. It is by virtue of it that the science of religions will escape dogmatism and stagnation.

The results of these two intellectual operations are equally valuable for a more adequate knowledge of *homo religiosus*. For, if the "phenomenologists" are interested in the meanings of religious data, the "historians," on their side, attempt to show how these meanings have been experienced and lived in the various cultures and historical moments, how they have been transformed, enriched, or impoverished in the course of history. But if we are to avoid sinking back into an obsolete "reductionism," this history of religious meanings must always be regarded as forming part of the history of the human spirit.[8]

More than any other humanistic discipline (i.e., psychology, anthropology, sociology, etc.), history of religions can open the way to a philosophical anthropology. For the sacred is a universal dimension and the beginnings of culture are rooted in religious experiences and beliefs. Furthermore, even after they are radically secularized, such cultural creations as social institutions, technology, moral ideas, arts, etc., cannot be correctly understood if one does not know their original religious matrix, which they tacitly criticized, modified, or rejected in becoming what they are now: secular cultural values. Thus, the historian of religions is in a position to grasp the permanence of what has been called man's specific existential situation of "being in the world," for the experience of the sacred is its correlate. In fact, man's becoming aware of his own mode of being and assuming his *presence* in the world together constitute a "religious" experience.

Ultimately, the historian of religions is forced by his hermeneutical endeavor to "relive" a multitude of existential situations and to unravel a number of presystematic ontologies. A historian of religions cannot say, for example, that he has understood the Australian religions if he has not understood the Australians' *mode of being in the world.* And as we shall see later on, even at that stage of culture we find the notion of a plurality of modes of being as well as the awareness that the singularity of the human condition is the result of a primordial "sacred history."

Now, these points cannot be successfully realized if the investigator does not understand that every religion has a *center,* in other words, a central conception which informs the entire corpus of myths, rituals, and beliefs. This is evident in such religions as Judaism, Christianity, and Islam, notwithstanding the fact that the modifications introduced in the course of time tend, in some cases, to obscure the "original form." For example, the central role of Jesus as Christ is transparent no matter how complex and elaborated some contemporary theological and ecclesiastical expressions may seem in comparison to "original Christianity." But the *center of a religion is not always so evident.* Some investigators do not even suspect that there is a *center;* rather, they try to articulate the religious values of a certain type of society in compliance with a fashionable theory. Thus, for almost three-quarters of a century the "primitive" religions were understood as illustrating one of the dominant theories of the day: animism, ancestor cult, *mana,* totemism, and so on. Australia, for example, was considered almost the territory par excellence of totemism, and because of the supposed archaism of the Australians, totemism was even proclaimed the most ancient form of religious life.

Whatever one may think of the various religious ideas and beliefs brought together under the name of "totemism," one thing seems evident today, namely, that totemism does *not* constitute the *center* of Australian religious life. On the contrary, the totemic expressions, as well as other religious ideas and beliefs, receive their full meaning and fall into a pattern only when the *center* of religious life is sought where the Australians have untiringly declared it to be: in the concept of the "Dreaming Time," that fabulous primordial epoch when the world was shaped and man became what he is today. We have discussed this problem at length elsewhere and it is unnecessary to take it up again here.[9]

This is only one example among many others, and perhaps not even the most illuminating, for the Australian religions do not present the complexity and the variety of forms that confront the student of Indian, Egyptian, or Greek religions. But it is easy to understand that the failure to search for the real *center* of a religion may explain the inadequate contributions made by the historians of religions to philosophical anthropology. . . . Such a shortcoming reflects a deeper and more complex crisis. But on the other hand, there are also signs that this crisis is in the process of being resolved.

Notes

1. Since "*Religionswissenschaft*" is not easily translatable into English, we are obliged to use "history of religions" in the broadest sense of the term, including not only history properly speaking but also the comparative study of religions and religious morphology and phenomenology.

2. Rudolph Otto described the sacred as the "*ganz andere.*" Although occurring on the nonreligious plane, the encounters with the "wholly other" brought about by depth psychology and modern artistic experiments can be reckoned as parareligious experiences.

3. It is also necessary to consider, for example, the vicissitudes of the work in the public consciousness, or even "unconscious." The circulation, assimilation, and evaluations of a literary work present problems that no discipline can solve by *itself.* It is the sociologist, but also the historian, the moralist, and the psychologist, who can help us to understand the success of *Werther* and the failure of *The Way of All Flesh,* the fact that such a difficult work as *Ulysses* became popular in less than twenty years, while *Senilità* and *Conscienza di Zeno* are still unknown, and so on.

4. We may even wonder if, at bottom, the various "reductionisms" do not betray the superiority complex of Western scholars. They have no doubt that only science—*an exclusively Western creation*—will resist this process of demystifying spirituality and culture.

5. M. Eliade, *Traité d'Histoire des Religions* (Paris: 1949), p. ii. English translation in *Patterns in Comparative Religions* (New York: 1958), p. xi.

6. Certain preliminary suggestions will be found in some of our preceding publications. See especially *Patterns in Comparative Religions,* pp. 1–33; *Images et Symboles* (Paris: 1951), pp. 33–52, 211–235 [English translation: *Images and Symbols* (New York: 1961), pp. 27–41, 16–78]; *Mythes, Rêves et Mystères* (Paris: 1957), pp. 7–15, 133–164 [English translation: *Myths, Dreams, and Mysteries* (New York: 1960), pp. 13–20, 99–122]; "Methodological Remarks on the Study of Religious Symbolism," in M. Eliade and Joseph M. Kitagawa, eds., *The History of Religions: Essays in Methodology* (Chicago: 1959), pp. 86–107.

7. These terms are used here in their broadest sense, including under "phenomenology" those scholars who pursue the study of structures and meanings, and under "history" those who seek to understand religious phenomena in their historical context. Actually, the divergences between these two approaches are more marked. In addition there are a certain number of differences—sometimes quite perceptible—within the groups that, for the sake of simplification, we have termed "phenomenologists" and "historians."

8. In one of his last works Raffaele Pettazzoni, the great historian of religions, reached similar conclusions. "Phenomenology and history complement each other. Phenomenology cannot do without ethnology, philology, and other historical disciplines. Phenomenology, on the other hand, gives the historical disciplines that sense of the religious which they are not able to capture. So conceived, religious phenomenology is the religious understanding (Verstandniss) of history; it is history in its religious dimension. Religious phenomenology and

history are not two sciences but are two complementary aspects of the integral science of religion, and the science of religion as such has a well-defined character given to it by its unique and proper subject matter." From "The Supreme Being: Phenomenological Structure and Historical Development," in M. Eliade and Joseph M. Kitagawa, eds., *History of Religions,* p. 66.

9. M. Eliade, "Australian Religion: An Introduction," *History of Religion,* 6 (1966):108–34, 208–37.

---------------§ℓ---------------

Sky, Moon, and Egg

These excerpts from Mircea Eliade's classic study of morphology in the history of religions, Patterns in Comparative Religion, *reveal his sensitivity to method as well as his interpretation of sky, moon, and egg as marvelous hierophanies.*

APPROXIMATIONS: THE STRUCTURE
AND MORPHOLOGY OF THE SACRED

1. "Sacred" and "Profane"

All the definitions given up till now of the religious phenomenon have one thing in common: Each has its own way of showing that the sacred and the religious life are the opposite of the profane and the secular life. But as soon as you start to fix limits to the notion of the sacred you come upon difficulties—difficulties both theoretical and practical. For, before you attempt any definition of the phenomenon of religion, you must know where to look for the evidence, and, first and foremost, for those expressions of religion that can be seen in the "pure state"—that is, those which are "simple" and as close as possible to their origins. Unfortunately, evidence of this sort is nowhere to be found; neither in any society whose history we know, nor among the "primitives," the uncivilized peoples of today. Almost everywhere the religious phenomena we see are complex, suggesting a long historical evolution.

Then, too, assembling one's material presents certain important practical difficulties. Even if one were satisfied with studying only one religion, a lifetime would scarcely be long enough to complete the

The selection "Sky, Moon, and Egg" is excerpted from Mircea Eliade's, *Patterns in Comparative Religion*, translated by Rosemary Sheed, World Publishing Co. (New York: Meridan Books, 1963). Excerpted passages appear on pages 1–7, 13–14, 38–40, 154–157, and 413–416.

research, while, if one proposed to compare religions, several lifetimes would not suffice to attain the end in view. Yet it is just such a comparative study that we want, for only thus can we discover both the changing morphology of the sacred, and its historical development. In embarking, therefore, on this study, we must choose a few among the many religions which have been discovered by history, or ethnology, and then only some of their aspects or phases.

This choice, even if confined to the major manifestations, is a delicate matter. If we want to limit and define the sacred, we shall have to have at our disposal a manageable number of expressions of religion. If it starts by being difficult, the diversity of those expressions becomes gradually paralyzing. We are faced with rites, myths, divine forms, sacred and venerated objects, symbols, cosmologies, theologoumena, consecrated men, animals and plants, sacred places, and more. And each category has its own morphology—of a branching and luxuriant richness. We have to deal with a vast and ill-assorted mass of material, with a Melanesian cosmogony myth or Brahman sacrifice having as much right to our consideration as the mystical writings of a St. Teresa or a Nichiren, an Australian totem, a primitive initiation rite, the symbolism of the Borobudur temple, the ceremonial costumes and dances of a Siberian shaman, the sacred stones to be found in so many places, agricultural ceremonies, the myths and rites of the Great Goddesses, the enthroning of an ancient king or the superstitions attaching to precious stones. Each must be considered as a hierophany in as much as it expresses in some way some modality of the sacred and some moment in its history; that is to say, some one of the many kinds of experience of the sacred man has had. Each is valuable for two things it tells us: because it is a hierophany, it reveals some modality of the sacred; because it is a historical incident, it reveals some attitude man has had towards the sacred. For instance, the following Vedic text addressing a dead man: "Crawl to your Mother, Earth! May she save you from the void!"[1] This text shows the nature of earth worship; the earth is looked upon as the Mother, *Tellus Mater*; but it also shows one given stage in the history of Indian religions, the moment when Mother Earth was valued—at least by one group—as a protectress against the void, a valuation which was to be done away with by the reform of the Upanishads and the preaching of Buddha.

To return to where we began, each category of evidence (myths, rites, gods, superstitions, and so on) is really equally important to us if we are to understand the religious phenomenon. And this understanding will always come about in relation to history. Every hierophany we look at is also an historical fact. Every manifestation of the sacred takes place in some historical situation. Even the most personal and transcendant mystical experiences are affected by the age in which they occur. The Jewish prophets owed a debt to the events of history, which justified them and confirmed their message; and also to the religious history of Israel, which made it possible for them to explain what they had experienced. As a historical phenomenon—though not as personal experience—the nihilism and ontologism of some of the Mahayana mystics would not have been possible without the Upanishad speculations, the evolution of Sanskrit and other things. I do not mean that every hierophany and every religious experience whatsoever is a unique and never-to-be-repeated incident in the working of the spirit. The greatest experiences are not only alike in content, but often also alike in their expression. Rudolf Otto discovered some astonishing similarities between the vocabulary and formulæ of Meister Eckhardt and those of Śaṅkara.

The fact that a hierophany is always an historical event (that is to say, always occurs in some definite situation) does not lessen its universal quality. Some hierophanies have a purely local purpose; others have, or attain, world-wide significance. The Indians, for instance, venerate a certain tree called *aśvattha*; the manifestation of the sacred in that particular plant species has meaning only for them, for only to them is the *aśvattha* anything more than just a tree. Consequently, that hierophany is not only of a certain time (as every hierophany must be), but also of a certain place. However, the Indians also have the symbol of a cosmic tree (*Axis Mundi*), and this mythico-symbolic hierophany is universal, for we find Cosmic Trees everywhere among ancient civilizations. But note that the *aśvattha* is venerated because it embodies the sacred significance of the universe in constant renewal of life; it is venerated, in fact, because it embodies, is part of, or symbolizes the universe as represented by all the Cosmic Trees in all mythologies. But although the *aśvattha* is explained by the same symbolism that we find in the Cosmic Tree, the hierophany which turns a particular plant-form into a sacred tree has a meaning only in the eyes of that particular Indian society.

To give a further example—in this case a hierophany which was left behind by the actual history of the people concerned: the Semites at one time in their history adored the divine couple made up of Ba'al, the god of hurricane and fecundity, and Belit, the goddess of fertility (particularly the fertility of the earth). The Jewish prophets held these cults to be sacrilegious. From their standpoint—from the standpoint, that is, of those Semites who had, as a result of the Mosaic reforms, reached a higher, purer and more complete conception of the Deity—such a criticism was perfectly justified. And yet the old Semitic cult of Ba'al and Belit *was* a hierophany: it showed (though in unhealthy and monstrous forms) the religious value of organic life, the elementary forces of blood, sexuality, and fecundity. This revelation maintained its importance, if not for thousands, at least for hundreds of years. As a hierophany it held sway till the time when it was replaced by another, which—completed in the religious experience of an élite—proved itself more satisfying and of greater perfection. The "divine form" of Yahweh prevailed over the "divine form" of Ba'al; it manifested a more perfect holiness, it sanctified life without in any way allowing to run wild the elementary forces concentrated in the cult of Ba'al, it revealed a spiritual economy in which man's life and destiny gained a totally new value; at the same time it made possible a richer religious experience, a communion with God at once purer and more complete. This hierophany of Yahweh had the final victory; because it represented a universal modality of the sacred, it was by its very nature open to other cultures; it became, by means of Christianity, of world-wide religious value. It can be seen, then, that some hierophanies are, or can in this way become, of universal value and significance, whereas others may remain local or of one period—they are not open to other cultures, and fall eventually into oblivion even in the society which produced them.

2. Difficulties of Method

But, to return to the great practical difficulty I mentioned earlier: the extreme diversity of the material we are faced with. To make matters worse, there seems no limit to the number of spheres whence we have drawn these hundreds of thousands of scraps of evidence. For one thing (as with all historical material), what we have at hand has survived more or less by chance (not merely in the case of written texts but also of monuments, inscriptions, oral traditions, and customs). For another, what has chanced to survive comes to us from many different sources. If, for instance, we want to piece together the early history of the Greek religion, we must make do with the very few texts that have come down to us, a few inscriptions, a few mutilated monuments, and some votive objects; in the case of the Germanic or Slavonic religions, we are obliged to make use of simple folklore, with the inevitable risks attaching to its handling and interpretation. A runic inscription, a myth recorded several centuries after it had ceased to be understood, a few symbolic pictures, a few protohistoric monuments, a mass of rites, and the popular legends of a century ago—nothing could be more ill-assorted than the material available to the historian of Germanic and Slavonic religion. Such a mixture of things would not be too bad if one were studying only one religion, but it is really serious when one attempts a comparative study of religions, or tries to grasp a great many different modalities of the sacred.

It is exactly as if a critic had to write a history of French literature with no other evidence than some fragments of Racine, a Spanish translation of La Bruyère, a few texts quoted by a foreign critic, the literary recollections of a few travellers and diplomats, the catalogue of a provincial library, the notes and exercise books of a schoolboy, and a few more hints of the same sort. That is really all the material available to a historian of religions: a few fragments from a vast oral priestly learning (the exclusive product of one social class), allusions found in travellers' notes, material gathered by foreign missionaries, reflections drawn from secular literature, a few monuments, a few inscriptions, and what memories remain in local traditions. All the historical sciences are, of course, tied to this sort of scrappy and accidental evidence. But the religious historian faces a bolder task than the historian, whose job is merely to piece together an event or a series of events with the aid of the few bits of evidence that are preserved to him; the religious historian must trace not only the *history* of a given hierophany, but must first of all understand and explain the modality of the sacred that that hierophany discloses. It would be difficult enough to interpret the meaning of a hierophany in any case, but the heterogeneous and chancy nature of the available evidence makes it far, far worse. Imagine a Buddhist trying to understand Christianity with only a few fragments of the Gospels, a Catholic breviary, various ornaments (Byzantine icons, Baroque statues of the saints, the vestments, perhaps, of an Orthodox priest), but able, on the other hand, to study the religious life of some European village. No doubt the first thing our Buddhist observer would note would be a distinct difference between the religious life of the peasants and the theological, moral, and mystical ideas of the village priest. But, while he would be quite right to note the distinction, he would be wrong if he refused to judge Christianity according to the traditions preserved by the priest on the grounds that he was merely a single individual—if he only held to be genuine the experience represented by the village as a community. The modalities of the sacred revealed by Christianity are in fact more truly preserved in the tradition represented by the priest (however strongly colored by history and theology) than in the beliefs of the villagers. What the observer is interested in is not the one moment in the history of Christianity, or one part of Christendom, but the Christian religion as such. The fact that only one man, in a whole village, may have a proper knowledge of Christian ritual, dogma, and mysticism, while the rest of the community are ill-informed about them and practice an elemental cult tinctured with superstition (with, that is, the remains of outworn hierophanies) does not, for his purpose at least, matter at all. What does matter is to realize that this single man has kept more completely, if not the original experience of Christianity, at least its basic elements and its mystical, theological, and ritual values.

We find this mistake in method often enough in ethnology. Paul Radin felt he had the right to reject the conclusions reached by the missionary Gusinde in his researches because his enquiries were limited to one man. Such an attitude would be justified only if the object of the enquiry were a strictly sociological one: if it were the religious life of a Fuegian community at a given time; but when it is a question of discovering what capacity the Fuegians have of experiencing religion, then the position is quite different. And the capacity of primitives to know different modalities of the sacred is one of the most important problems of religious history. Indeed, if one can show (as has been done in recent decades) that the religious lives of the most primitive peoples are in fact complex, that they cannot be reduced to "animism," "totemism," or even ancestor-worship, that they include visions of Supreme Beings with all the powers of an omnipotent Creator-God, then these evolutionist hypotheses which deny the primitive any approach to "superior hierophanies" are nullified. . . .

5. The Dialectic of Hierophanies

I mentioned at the beginning of this chapter that all the definitions that have ever been given of the religious phenomenon make the sacred the opposite of the profane. What I have just said—that anything whatever can become at any given moment a hierophany—may seem to contradict all these definitions. If anything whatever may embody separate values, can the sacred-profane dichotomy have any meaning? The contradiction is, in fact, only a surface one, for while it is true that anything at all can become a hierophany, and that in all probability there is nothing that has not, somewhere, some time, been invested with a sacred value, it still remains that no one religion or race has ever been found to contain all these hierophanies in its history. In other words, in every religious framework there have always been profane beings and things beside the sacred. (The same cannot be said of physiological actions, trades, skills, gestures and so on, but I shall come to this distinction later.) Further: while a certain class of things may be found fitting vehicles of the sacred, there always remain some things in the class which are not given this honor.

For instance, in the so-called "worship of stones" not all stones are held to be sacred. We shall always find that *some* stones are venerated because they are a certain shape, or because they are very large, or because they are bound up with some ritual. Note, too, that it is not a question of actually worshipping the stones; the stones are venerated precisely because they are not simply stones but hierophanies, something outside their normal status as things. The dialectic of a hierophany implies a more or less clear choice, a singling-out. A thing becomes sacred in so far as it embodies (that is, reveals) something other than itself. Here we need not be concerned with whether that something other comes from its unusual shape, its efficacy, or simply its "power"— or whether it springs from the thing's fitting in with some symbolism or other, or has been given it by some rite of consecration, or acquired by its being placed in some position that is instinct with sacredness (a sacred zone, a sacred time, some "accident"—a thunderbolt, crime, sacrilege or such). What matters is that a hierophany implies a *choice*, a clear-cut separation of this thing which manifests the sacred from everything else around it. There is always something *else*, even when it is some whole sphere that becomes sacred—the sky, for instance, or a certain familiar landscape, or the "fatherland." The thing that becomes sacred is still separated in regard to itself, for it only becomes a hierophany at the moment of stopping to be a mere profane something, at the moment of acquiring a new "dimension" of sacredness. . . .

THE SKY AND SKY GODS

11. *The Sacredness of the Sky*

The most popular prayer in the world is addressed to "Our Father who art in heaven." It is possible that man's earliest prayers were addressed to the same heavenly father—it would explain the testimony of an African of the Ewe tribe: "There where the sky is, God is too." The Vienna school of ethnology (particularly in the person of Fr. W. Schmidt, the author of the fullest monograph yet produced on the subject of the origins of the idea of divinity) even claims to have established the existence of a primitive monotheism, basing the proof chiefly on the belief in sky gods among the most primitive human societies. For the moment we will leave on one side this problem of primeval monotheism. What is quite beyond doubt is that there is an almost universal belief in a celestial divine being, who created the universe and guarantees the fecundity of the earth (by pouring rain down upon it). These beings are endowed with infinite foreknowledge and wisdom; moral laws and often tribal ritual as well were established by them during a brief visit to the earth; they watch to see that their laws are obeyed, and lightning strikes all who infringe them.

We shall look at a series of divine figures of the sky, but first it is necessary to grasp the religious significance of the sky as such. There is no need to look into the teachings of myth to see that the sky itself

directly reveals a transcendence, a power, and a holiness. Merely contemplating the vault of heaven produces a religious experience in the primitive mind. This does not necessarily imply a "nature-worship" of the sky. To the primitive, nature is never purely "natural." The phrase "contemplating the vault of heaven" really means something when it is applied to primitive man, receptive to the miracles of every day to an extent we find it hard to imagine. Such contemplation is the same as a revelation. The sky shows itself as it really is: infinite, transcendent. The vault of heaven is, more than anything else, "something quite apart" from the tiny thing that is man and his span of life. The symbolism of its transcendence derives from the simple realization of its infinite height. "Most High" becomes quite naturally an attribute of the divinity. The regions above man's reach, the starry places, are invested with the divine majesty of the transcendent, of absolute reality, of everlastingness. Such places are the dwellings of the gods; certain privileged people go there as a result of rites effecting their ascension into heaven; there, according to some religions, go the souls of the dead. The "high" is something inaccessible to man as such; it belongs by right to superhuman powers and beings; when a man ceremonially ascends the steps of a sanctuary, or the ritual ladder leading to the sky he ceases to be a man; the souls of the privileged dead leave their human state behind when they rise into heaven.

All this derives from simply contemplating the sky; but it would be a great mistake to see it as a logical, rational process. The transcendental quality of "height," or the supra-terrestrial, the infinite, is revealed to man all at once, to his intellect as to his soul as a whole. The symbolism is an immediate notion of the whole consciousness, of the man, that is, who realizes himself as a man, who recognizes his place in the universe; these primeval realizations are bound up so organically with his life that the same symbolism determines both the activity of his subconscious and the noblest expressions of his spiritual life. It really is important, therefore, this realization that though the symbolism and religious values of the sky are not deduced logically from a calm and objective observation of the heavens, neither are they exclusively the product of mythical activity and non-rational religious experience. Let me repeat: even before any religious values have been set upon the sky it reveals its transcendence. The sky "symbolizes" transcendence, power, and changelessness simply by being there. It exists because it is high, infinite, immovable, powerful.

That the mere fact of being high, of being high up, means being powerful (in the religious sense), and being as such filled with the sacred, is shown by the very etymology of some of the gods' names. To the Iroquois, all that has *orenda* is called *oki*, but the meaning of the word *oki* seems to be "what is on high"; we even find a Supreme Being of the sky called Oke.[2] The Sioux express magico-religious power by the word *wakan*, which is phonetically extremely close to *wakan*, *wankan*, which means, in the Dakota language, "on high, above"; the sun, the moon, lightning, the wind, possess *wakan*, and this force was personified though imperfectly in "Wakan," which the missionaries translated as meaning "Lord," but who was in fact a Supreme Being of the sky, manifesting himself above all in lightning.[3]

The supreme divinity of the Maoris is called Iho: *iho* means "raised up, on high."[4] The Akposo negroes have a Supreme God Uwoluwu; the name means "what is on high, the upper regions."[5] And one could multiply these examples.[6] We shall see soon that "the most high," "the shining," "the sky," are notions which have existed more or less explicitly in the terms used by primitive civilizations to express the idea of Godhead. The transcendence of God is directly revealed in the inaccessibility, infinity, eternity, and creative power (rain) of the sky. The whole nature of the sky is an inexhaustible hierophany. Consequently, anything that happens among the stars or in the upper areas of the atmosphere—the rhythmic revolution of the stars, chasing clouds, storms, thunderbolts, meteors, rainbows—is a moment in that hierophany.

When this hierophany became personified, when the divinities *of* the sky showed themselves, or took the place of the holiness of the sky as such, is difficult to say precisely. What is quite certain is that the sky divinities have always been supreme divinities; that their hierophanies, dramatized in various ways by myth, have remained for that reason sky hierophanies; and that what one may call the history of sky divinities is largely a history of notions of "force," of "creation," of "laws," and of "sovereignty." . . .

THE MOON AND ITS MYSTIQUE

47. The Moon and Time

The sun is always the same, always itself, never in any sense "becoming." The moon, on the other hand, is a body which waxes, wanes, and disappears, a body whose existence is subject to the universal law of becoming, of birth and death. The moon, like man, has a career involving tragedy, for its failing, like man's, ends in death. For three nights the starry sky is without a moon. But this "death" is followed by a rebirth: the "new moon." The moon's going out, in "death," is never final. One Babylonian hymn to Sin sees the moon as "a fruit growing from itself."[7] It is reborn of its own substance, in pursuance of its own destined career.

This perpetual return to its beginnings, and this ever-recurring cycle make the moon *the* heavenly body above all others concerned with the rhythms of life. It is not surprising, then, that it governs all those spheres of nature that fall under the law of recurring cycles: waters, rain, plant life, fertility. The phases of the moon showed man time in the concrete sense—as distinct from astronomical time which certainly only came to be realized later. Even in the Ice Age the meaning of the moon's phases and their magic powers were clearly known. We find the symbolism of spirals, snakes, and lightning—all of them growing out of the notion of the moon as the measure of rhythmic change and fertility—in the Siberian cultures of the Ice Age.[8] Time was quite certainly measured everywhere by the phases of the moon. Even today there are nomad tribes living off what they can hunt and grow who use only the lunar calendar. The oldest Indo-Aryan root connected with the heavenly bodies is the one that means "moon":[9] it is the root *me*, which in Sanskrit becomes *māmi*, "I measure." The moon becomes the universal measuring gauge. All the words relating to the moon in the Indo-European languages come from that root: *mās* (Sanskrit), *mah* (Avestic), *mah* (Old Prussian), *menu* (Lithuanian), *mena* (Gothic), *mene* (Greek), *mensis* (Latin). The Germans used to measure time by nights.[10] Traces of this ancient way of reckoning are also preserved in popular European traditions; certain feasts are celebrated at night as, for instance, Christmas night, Easter, Pentecost, Saint John's Day and so on.[11]

Time as governed and measured by the phases of the moon might be called "living" time. It is bound up with the reality of life and nature, rain and the tides, the time of sowing, the menstrual cycle. A whole series of phenomena belonging to totally different "cosmic levels" are ordered according to the rhythms of the moon or are under their influence. The "primitive mind," once having grasped the "powers" of the moon, then establishes connections of response and even interchange between the moon and those phenomena. Thus, for instance, from the earliest times, certainly since the Neolithic Age, with the discovery of agriculture, the same symbolism has linked together the moon, the sea waters, rain, the fertility of women and of animals, plant life, man's destiny after death, and the ceremonies of initiation. The mental syntheses made possible by the realization of the moon's rhythms connect and unify very varied realities; their structural symmetries and the analogies in their workings could never have been seen had not "primitive" man intuitively perceived the moon's law of periodic change, as he did very early on.

The moon measures, but it also unifies. Its "forces" or rhythms are what one may call the "lowest common denominator" of an endless number of phenomena and symbols. The whole universe is seen as a pattern, subject to certain laws. The world is no longer an infinite space filled with the activity of a lot of disconnected autonomous creatures: within that space itself things can be seen to correspond and fit together. All this, of course, is not the result of a reasoned analysis of reality, but of an ever clearer intuition of it in its totality. Though there may be a series of ritual or mythical side-commentaries on the moon which are separate from the rest, with their own somewhat specialized function (as, for instance, certain mythical lunar beings with only one foot or one hand, by whose magic power one can cause rain to fall), there can be no symbol, ritual, or myth of the moon that does not imply all the lunar values known at a given time. There can be no part without the whole. The spiral, for instance, which was taken to be a symbol of the moon as early as the Ice Age, relates to the phases of the moon, but also includes erotic elements springing from the vulva-shell analogy, water elements (the moon=shell), and some to do with fertility (the double volute, horns, and so on). By wearing a pearl as an amulet a women is united to the powers of water (shell), the moon (the shell a symbol of the moon; created by the rays of the moon, etc.), eroticism, birth, and embryology. A medicinal plant contains in itself the threefold effectiveness of the moon, the waters, and vegetation, even when only one of these powers is explicitly present in the mind of the user. Each of these powers or "effectivenesses" in its turn works on a number of different levels. Vegetation, for instance, implies notions of death and rebirth, of light and darkness (as zones of the universe), of fecundity and abundance, and so on. There is no such thing as a symbol, emblem, or power with only one kind of meaning. Everything hangs together, everything is connected, and makes up a cosmic whole. . . .

157. *The Cosmogonic Egg*

A creation myth of the Society Islands tells of Ta'aroa, "ancestor of all the gods" and creator of the universe, sitting "in his shell in darkness from eternity. The shell was like an egg revolving in endless space."[12] This motif of the cosmogonic egg which we find in Polynesia[13] is also common to ancient India,[14] Indonesia,[15] Iran, Greece,[16] Phœnicia,[17] Latvia, Estonia, Finland,[18] the Pangwe of West Africa,[19] Central America, and the west coast of South America (according to Frobenius' map).[20] The center from which this myth originated is probably to be located in India or Indonesia. What are specially important to us are the ritual or mythological parallels of the cosmogonic egg; in Oceania, for instance, it is believed that man is born of an egg;[21] in other words, the creation of the cosmos here serves as a model for the creation of man, the creation of man copies and repeats that of the cosmos.

Then, too, in a great many places the egg is connected with the symbols and emblems of the renovation of nature and vegetation; the new year trees, Maypoles, Saint John's trees, and so on, are decorated with eggs or eggshells.[22] We know that all these emblems of vegetation and the New Year in some way sum up the myth of periodic creation. The tree is itself a symbol of nature and her unwearying renewal, and when the egg is added to it, it confirms all these cosmogonic values. Hence the major role it plays in the East in all the new year dramas. In Persia, for instance, colored eggs are the appropriate gifts for the New Year which, even today, is still called the Feast of Red Eggs.[23] And the red eggs given at Easter in the Balkan countries are probably also left over from a similar ritual pattern used to celebrate the coming of spring.

In all these cases, as in those we are coming to, the ritual power of the egg cannot be explained by any empirical or rationalist interpretation of the egg looked upon as a seed: it is founded on the symbol embodied in the egg, which bears not so much upon birth as upon a *rebirth* modelled on the creation of the world. Otherwise there could be no explanation for the important place eggs hold in the celebration of the New Year and the feasts of the dead. We have already seen the close connection between the cult of the dead and the start of the year; at the New Year, when the world is recreated, the dead feel themselves drawn toward the living and can hope, up to a point, to return to life. Whichever of these ritual and mythological patterns we turn to, the basic idea is not that of ordinary birth, but rather the *repeating of the archetypal birth* of the cosmos, the imitation of the cosmogony. During the Hindu vegetation feast, Holi, which is also a feast of the dead, the custom in some places is to light fires and cast into them two little statuettes, one of a man, the other of a woman, representing Kāmadeva and Rati; with the first statuette an egg and a living hen are also thrown on to the fire.[24] When it takes this form, the feast symbolises the death and resurrection of Kāmadeva and Rati. The egg strengthens and assists the resurrection which, again, is not a birth, but a "return," a "repetition."

We find symbolism of this sort even in some prehistoric and proto-historic societies. Clay eggs have been found in a great many tombs in Russia and in Sweden;[25] with good reason Arne sees them as emblems of immortality. In the ritual of Osiris, various ingredients (diamond-dust, fig flour, aromatic spices, and so on) are shaped into an egg—though we do not yet fully apprehend for what function.[26] The statues of Dionysos found in Bœotian tombs all have an egg in one hand to symbolize a return to life.[27] This explains the Orphic prohibition against eating eggs,[28] for the prime object of Orphism was to escape from the unending cycle of reincarnation—to abolish, in other words, the periodic return to life.

I will conclude with a few other instances of how the egg is used in ritual. There is, first, its role in the agricultural rituals still in use in modern times. To ensure that the grain would grow, Finnish peasants used to keep an egg in their pockets throughout the time of sowing, or place an egg in the ploughed earth.[29] The Estonians eat eggs during ploughing time "to have strength," and the Swedes throw eggs down on ploughed fields. When the Germans are sowing flax they sometimes put eggs with it, or put an egg in the field, or eat eggs during the time of sowing.[30] The Germans still have the custom of burying blessed Easter eggs in their fields.[31] The Cheremisses and the Votyaks throw eggs up in the air before they start their sowing;[32] on other occasions they would bury an egg among the furrows as an offering to the Earth Mother.[33] The egg is at once an offering to the gods of the underworld and an offering used frequently in the cult of the dead.[34] But whatever ritual pattern it is linked with, the egg never loses its primary meaning: it ensures the *repetition* of the act of creation which gave birth *in illo tempore* to living forms. When they pick a simple, some people put an egg on the spot to ensure that another herb will grow there in its place.[35]

Notes

1. *Ṛg Veda*. bk. x: 18, 10.
2. R. Pettazzoni, *Dio* vol. 1 (Rome: 1922), p. 310. All references to Pettazzoni's work are to Volume 1; Volume 2 has not appeared. Schmidt, *Der Ursprung der Gottesidee* Vol. 2, (Munster: 1926), p. 399.
3. Pettazzoni, pp. 290ff; Schmidt, Vol. 2, pp. 402, 648–652.
4. Pettazzoni, p. 175.
5. Pettazzoni, p. 244.
6. Cf. Pettazzoni, p. 358, n2.
7. Furlani, *La Religione babilonese-assira,* Vol. 1 (Bologna: 1929), p. 155.
8. E.g., at Irkutsk; cf. Hentze, *Mythes et symboles lunaires* (Antwerp: 1932), pp. 84ff., figs. 59, 60.
9. Cf. Schrader, *Sprachvergleichung und Urgeschichte,* 2nd ed. (Jena: 1883), pp. 443ff.; W. Schultz, "Zeitrechnung und Weltordnung," *Mannus-Bibliotek* no. 35 (Leipzig: 1924):12ff.
10. Tacitus, *Germania,* vol. ii.
11. Kuhn, quoted in Hentze, p. 248.
12. Handy, *Polynesian Religion* (Honolulu: 1927), p. 12.
13. Cf. Dixon, *Oceanic Mythology* (Boston: 1916), p. 20.
14. *Śatapatha-Br.,* pp. xi, 1, 6, 1ff; *Laws of Manu,* pp. 1, 5ff., etc.
15. Numazawa, *Die Weltänfange in der japanischen Mythologie* (Lucerne-Paris: 1946), p. 310; Krappe, *Mythologie Universel* (Paris: 1930), p. 397.
16. Harrison, *Prolegomena to the Study of Greek Religion,* 3rd ed. (Cambridge: 1922), pp. 627ff.
17. Numazawa, p. 309.
18. Numazawa, p. 310; Krappe, p. 414.
19. Krappe, p. 371, n1.
20. Reproduced by W. Liungman in "Traditionswanderungen: Euphrat-Rhein," I, in *Folklore Fellowship Communications,* Volumes 1 and 2 (Helsinki: 1937–1938), pp. 118–119.
21. Indonesia, Dixon, p. 160, pp. 169ff.; Melanesia, Dixon, p. 109; Polynesia, Micronesia, Dixon, p. 109, n17.
22. Mannhardt, *Baumkultus* pp. 244ff.; pp. 263 ff., etc.
23. Lassy, *Muharram Mysteries* (Helsinki: 1916), pp. 219ff.; Liungman, "Euphrat-Rhein," I, p. 20.
24. Crooke, "The Holi: A Vernal Festival of the Hindus," in *Folklore,* Vol. 25, 75.
25. T. J. Arne, *La Suède et l'Orient* (Uppsala: 1914), p. 216.
26. Liungman, "Euphrat-Rhein," I, pp. 141ff.
27. Nilsson, *Geschichte der griechischen Religion* (Munich: 1941), vol. 1, p. 565.
28. Rohde, *Psyche* (London: 1925), p. 357, n2; Harrison, p. 629.
29. Rantasalo, "Der Ackerbau in Volksaberglauben der Finnen und Esten mit entsprechenden Gebräuchen der Germanen verglichen," in *Folklore Fellowship Communications,* no. 32 (Helsinki: 1919–1925), pp. 55–56.

30. Rantasalo, p. 57.
31. Rantasalo, p. 58.
32. Rantasalo, p. 58.
33. Holmberg-Harva, *Die Religion der Tcheremissen* (Porvoo: 1926), p. 179.
34. M. Nilsson, "Das Ei im Totenkult der Alten," in *Archiv für Religions-wissenschaft* (1908), p. xi.
35. Delatte, *Herbarius* (Liège-Paris: 1938), p. 120.

—§2—

Vocation and Destiny:
Savant, Not Saint

This selection from the Autobiography *recounts Eliade's awareness at the age of twenty-three of his vocation and destiny.*

Neither the life of an "adopted Bengalese" nor that of a Himalayan hermit would have allowed me to fulfill the possibilities with which I had come into the world. Sooner or later I should have awakened from my "Indian existence"—historical or transhistorical—and it would have been difficult to return, because by that time I should not have been only twenty-three. What I had tried to do—renounce my Western culture and seek a "home" or a "world" in an exotic spiritual universe— was equivalent in a sense to a premature renunciation of all my creative potentialities. I could not have been creative except by remaining in *my* world—which in the first place was the world of Romanian language and culture. And I had no right to renounce it until I had done my duty to it: that is, until I had exhausted my creative potential. I should have the right to withdraw permanently to the Himalayas at the *end* of my cultural activities, but not at the beginning of them. To believe that I could, at twenty-three, sacrifice history and culture for "the Absolute" was further proof that I had not understood India. My vocation was culture, not sainthood. I ought to have known that I had no right to "skip steps" and renounce cultural creativity except in the case of a special vocation—which I did not have. But of course I understood all this only later. . . .

From *Autobiography: Volume I: 1907–1937, Journey East, Journey West*, 199–201, 204. Reprinted with permission of Harper & Row and the author.

I have felt ever since then that this period was different from the other phases of my life in India. I found other friends, I frequented other places, I was engaged with other problems. After the lessons I had learned in Bhawanipore and Svarga Ashram, I turned instinctively toward other springs of that inexhaustible India. From then on I no longer tried to become a different person, imitating an Indian model, but I let myself be drawn by the mystery of the many obscure or neglected aspects of Indian culture. . . .

But there was something else that made me feel an urgency to understand Indian spirituality and Asian culture in general. I knew that Indian independence was imminent, and that very shortly the whole of Asia would reenter history. On the other hand, in the not-so-distant future a number of archaic peoples would take their places on the stage of world politics. It seemed to me that we Romanians could fulfill a definite role in the coming dialogue between the two or three worlds: the West, Asia, and cultures of the archaic folk type. To me it appeared useless to repeat certain Western clichés or discoveries—but likewise it seemed sterile and dangerous to take a stand in an antiquated "traditionalism." It was precisely the peasant roots of a good part of our Romanian culture that compelled us to transcend nationalism and cultural provincialism and to aim for "universalism." The common elements of Indian, Balkan, and Mediterranean folk culture proved to me that it is *here* that organic universalism exists, that it is the result of a common history (the history of peasant cultures) and not an abstract construct. We, the people of Eastern Europe, would be able to serve as a bridge between the West and Asia. A good part of my activity in Romania between 1932 and 1940 found its point of departure in these intuitions and observations made in the spring and summer of 1931.

Literature and Fantasy

"Literature and Fantasy" is an excerpt from the Foreword to Mircea Eliade's recently published Tales of the Sacred and the Supernatural, *displaying his view of the meaning of art.*

That which characterizes us as human and defines us vis-à-vis other orders of nature and God is the instinct for transcendence, the craving to be freed from oneself and to pass over into the other, the urgent need to break the iron band of individuality. Dream, the safety valve of this thirst for transcendence, as well as art, magic, dance, and love and mysticism—these all testify from various angles to the fundamental and fated instinct of human nature for emergence from oneself and fusion with the other, for a flight from limited solitariness and a bounding toward perfect freedom in the freedom of the other.

It seems to me that art is nothing other than a magical transcendence of the object, its projection into another dimension, its liberation through magical realization and creativity. This dimension is difficult to specify, but the intuition of it provokes what is called an aesthetic thrill, which is really nothing but a magical joy at the victorious bursting of the iron band.

It is, I say, the joy felt by the one who contemplates it over the fact that someone else, the artist, has succeeded in circumventing human fate, has succeeded in creating. It is the religious thrill of the *creature*, but with this difference: while the creature-feeling which we experience in any religious thrill reveals our dependence on God as one of God's creatures, in the case of the artistic thrill the predominant sentiment is

"Literature and Fantasy" is an excerpt from the author's foreword to his collection of short stories *Tales of the Sacred and the Supernatural* (Philadelphia: Westminster Press, 1981). It is reprinted here with permission of the publishers and the author.

something else: the joy that a *human being* has created, has imitated God's work, has been saved from a destined sterility, has breached those walls of impotence and finitude. On the one hand there is the formula "I am created by God," which inevitably arouses the consciousness of nothingness, of religious fear, of the taste of dust and ashes. On the other hand there is the statement "A human being, like myself, has created, like God," which brings the joy that a fellow creature has imitated creation, has become a demiurge, a force in the creating. That is why one finds so often the spirit of magic in a work of art: it is a projection, through the will and the genius, both magical in nature, of the inner world, the drama of individuality, in a dimension little accessible to the everyday consciousness, but realized and experienced through the artistic act. . . .

The tragic fate, which only a few realize in all its depths, of not being able to go out of yourself except by losing yourself, of not being able to communicate soul to soul (because any communication is illusory, except for love, which is a communion), of remaining terrified and alone in a world which in appearance is so osmotic, so intimate—that tragic fate can only incite an unwearying struggle against itself, an immensely varied combat in opposition to its laws. Hence the magical, artistic impulse of genius which cries that the law is for others, while play and fantasy are for the demon in us, for the artist and the dreamer. We are conditioned by creation and are ourselves created. But that creative and self-revealing instinct transcends creation. We create! We ignore the law and are beyond good and evil. We create through play, and we realize that dimension of dream wherein we enjoy absolute freedom, where the categories of existence are ignored and fate is suppressed. Any revolt against the laws of fate must have the character of play, of the divine. . . .

The magical structure of play and fantasy is obvious. In its "leap" it creates a new space with a centrifugal motion, in the center of which stands, as it were, the demiurge, the creative force of a new cosmos. From it, from this actualization of primordiality, everything begins. This leap *outside* indicates the beginning of a new world. It matters little that this world will find its own new laws quickly, laws over which new others will be unable to pass. It remains a magical, demiurgical creation, just as a work of art is a creation even if, when completed, it falls under the domination of physical, social, economic, or artistic laws.

A Terrific Illusionist:
The Best!

This incredible excerpt from The Old Man and the Bureaucrats *is a specific example of Eliade's capacity to turn fantasy into literature.*

"Ah," smiled Farama, "this is a long story. I wrote out part of it the day before yesterday. I don't know if you've had the opportunity to look over what I wrote. Her father let her go because that year the *Doftor* came again to see the forester, and this *Doftor* was endowed with strange powers."

"The Doctor? Doctor who? What was his name?"

"Only the forester knew what his real name was because he had known him as a child. People called him the *Doftor* because of his skill with all kinds of cures, and because he was always traveling in foreign lands, far away. He knew many languages, countless sciences, and he cured people and cattle with simple old wives' remedies, but his great weakness was performing feats of magic. He was unsurpassed at sleight-of-hand and he was also an illusionist, a fakir, and God knows what else, for he did incredible things. All this he did for his own pleasure and only at country fairs and small market towns, never at Bucuresti. This is what he loved best to do—take several children with him in two carts with six horses, and wander for a month or two through the villages between Saint Petru and Saint Maria. That year he took with him Oana, Lixandru, Aldea, and Ionescu. They set out for Campulung and from there they headed for the mountains, but they couldn't go up

This selection from *The Old Man and the Bureaucrats*, translated by Mac Linscott Ricketts (Notre Dame: Notre Dame University Press, 1980), is reprinted here with permission from the publishers and the author.

the mountain because in the meantime Romania entered the war. . . .
A great conjuror!" Farama exclaimed, shaking his head.

"Did you go to see him?"

"I saw him several times—at work, I mean, at his conjuring. The first time was at the forester's, in his yard—and I just couldn't believe it! It was on a Sunday toward evening and we were waiting for the horses to be harnessed to the carriage so we could go home. There were about ten of us and we all had business in Bucuresti the next day. 'Stay a little longer and I'll show you something!' cried the *Doftor*, clapping his hands for silence. Then he began to walk back and forth in front of us with his hands in his pockets, frowning, thoughtful. Suddenly he lifted one hand and grasped something from the air. We looked at it closely and saw that it was a kind of thin thread of glass. He laid it on the ground and began to pull it and stretch it, and the thread soon became a pane about a meter and a half square, which he made fast in the ground, then seized one side and again began to pull and stretch it out behind him. In about two or three minutes he had made a glass reservoir several meters in size, a kind of enormous aquarium. Then we saw the water gush up powerfully from the earth and fill the tank to the brim. The *Doftor* made a few more motions and we saw many kinds of fish, large and brightly colored, swimming in the water. We were astounded. The *Doftor* lit a cigarette and turned to us, saying, 'Come closer. Examine the fish and tell me which one you want me to get for you.' We approached and indicated a large fish with a blue crest and red eyes. 'Ha!' said the *Doftor* 'You've chosen well. This is *Ichthys Columbarius*, a rare fish from the South Seas.' And without removing the cigarette from his mouth he walked right through the glass like a shadow, and into the tank. He stayed there in the middle of it, in the water among the fish, for some time, where we could all see him perfectly. He walked around with the cigarette still burning between his lips, then he stretched out his hand and seized the *Columbarius*. He came out of the tank just as he'd entered it, passing through the glass with the cigarette in the corner of his mouth, and in his hands he held the fish, which he showed to us. We watched it struggle, but we were more interested in the *Doftor*. He didn't have a drop of water on him—not on his face nor on his clothes. One of the men took the fish in his hand, but it escaped immediately into the grass and we all leaped to catch it. The *Doftor* laughed. He captured the fish, put his hand through the glass of the tank and let the creature go free in the water. Then he clapped his hands, and the aquarium with the fish and all disappeared. . . ."

"Great illusionist!" exclaimed the man at the desk.

"The greatest! But this—what I'm telling you now—was nothing compared with what he used to do at the markets and fairs, especially that summer when he took Oana and the boys with him. You can imagine that after I'd seen him at Paserea I had no other thought than to see him again. I followed them in the train to Domnesti, about forty kilometers from Campulung, where there was a large cattle market. We stayed five days in all. He did conjuring tricks two or three times a day and they were never the same, and he changed the ceremony each time, too. He especially liked to do things in great style, real gala performances. The first day Lixandru appeared on a white horse, clothed like a prince, and he wandered all around the marketplace without uttering a word. I say it was Lixandru because I knew him and I'd talked with him in the morning. Otherwise I shouldn't have recognized him, because first of all the *Doftor* had changed him on that day. He'd made him taller and stronger, like a young man of twenty, and his hair was thick and fell in long locks down his back, the way men wore it in former times. And his face—although strictly speaking the *Doftor* hadn't changed it—still, it no longer seemed to be his face because he was much more handsome and he had a different expression—profound, noble, melancholy. How can I describe how he was dressed, and what a horse he rode? Everybody followed him—several hundred people—

and stayed with him all the way to the *Doftor*'s tent. It was huge, such as only the big circuses in the cities were accustomed to use. How the *Doftor* carried it in the two carts in which he roamed through the villages I never understood. And there in front of the tent Ionescu was waiting for them, also transformed so you could no longer recognize him. He was tall and fat and black, thick-lipped like a blackamoor, dressed in full trousers, his torso naked, with a scimitar in his hand, and he shouted, 'Come in! We're working to get a dowry for Oana!' And when they entered the tent Aldea greeted them, seated at an elegant table with gold feet, surrounded by sacks of ducats. 'Five *bani!** Five *bani!*' he shouted, 'but we'll give you change!' The people gave him five *bani* and received a ducat in change. 'But of course you know they're no longer good. They're not a medium of exchange, now,' Aldea told them, thrusting his hand into the sack and counting out the ducats.

"Great illusionist!" cried the man behind the desk.

"Very great!" Farama agreed. "I looked into the sacks of ducats. 'They're no longer a medium of exchange, *domnule* Principal,' Aldea said. And really, there were *thalers* from the time of Maria Theresia

---

*Smallest Romanian monetary unit: one *ban*.

and ducats from Peter the Great, and many Turkish coins. But this was nothing compared to what was to come. When the tent was full of people the *Doftor* appeared from behind a curtain in formal attire, with white gloves, with a mustache that was long and thin and very black. He clapped his hands and Oana came out from behind the curtain. She alone was just as I knew her to be. She seemed unchanged, though she was dressed differently, in a skin-tight white jersey. She looked like a statue. Then the *Doftor* raised his hand high and took from the air a little box no bigger than a pillbox, which he began to stretch so that it grew larger before our very eyes. He continued to tug it, now on one side, then on the other, on the bottom and on the top, until he made a chest of about two meters in length and approximately the same dimensions in breadth and depth. Then he took it and gave it to Oana to hold in both hands as high as she could reach above her head. Now, as Oana stood motionless, holding the chest up in the air with both hands, she resembled a statue more than ever. She looked like a caryatid. The *Doftor* stepped back and eyed her with satisfaction, then reached up again and took out of the air a box of matches. He removed some from the box and stretched them—lengthened them, broadened them— until he made a stairway which he propped against the chest. Then he turned to the audience and announced, 'Will the authorities please step forward?' And when no one ventured to approach he began to call them by name, as though he had always known them: '*Domnule* Mayor, please! *Domnule* Mayor, *doamna* Mayoress, bring Ionel with you, too. . . . And *domnule* Police Chief, please! Sergeant-Major Namolosu! And you come too, *domnule* teacher so-and-so. . . .' In this way, one after another, he addressed each one and invited him to come out of the crowd. Taking them by the hand, he urged them to climb the stairs and enter the chest. The people were rather hesitant, but once they reached the top, in front of the door, they were ashamed to turn back and they went in. Thus the Mayor and his wife entered, and their son Ionel, the teacher, the Police Chief, and then the assistant to the Mayor with his whole family—he had come with three sisters-in-law, each with several children—and then the other people followed in no special order, as the *Doftor* invited them, calling them by name. About thirty or forty more went in like that, and finally he caught sight of the priest, who had just arrived, and stepping forward the *Doftor* invited him. 'Please, your Reverence, you come too. . . .' At first the priest didn't want to. 'What kind of deviltry is this, *Doftore?*' he demanded. 'What are you doing to these people?' 'Come, your Reverence, and you'll see!'

"So the priest, who was old and walked with some difficulty—but was otherwise handsome and robust—climbed the stairs slowly and disappeared in the chest too. Oana had not moved in all this time. She might have been holding a kerchief in her hands. After he saw the priest enter the chest the *Doftor* climbed the stairs and began to manipulate it. He squeezed it, he pressed it, first on the sides, then from top to bottom, until it was reduced by half. Then he came down with it in his arms and in front of the crowd he again began to press it and make it more compact, and in a few minutes the chest had become what it was in the beginning—a little pillbox. Then he took it between his fingers, spun it around several times until he made it as tiny as a pea and he asked, 'Who wants it?' And an old man replied from the back, 'Give it to me, *Doftore*, all my grandchildren are in it!' And the *Doftor* flicked it with his fingernail, but it was so tiny that as soon as he tossed it away, it vanished, and the next moment we heard a 'pop' and everybody—the priest and the mayor and all the others—were again in their places, each where he had been before. . . ."

"Terrific illusionist!"

"Unprecedented!" agreed Farama, nodding his head, "but this—what I just told you—is nothing compared with what happened at Campulung.

---§℘---

The Terror of History

"The Terror of History," from Eliade's widely read Myth of the Eternal Return, *is one of his most provocative and controversial statements about the nature of "historicism" in the modern era.*

Survival of the Myth of Eternal Return

The problem raised in this final chapter exceeds the limits that we had assigned to the present essay. Hence we can only outline it. In short, it would be necessary to confront "historical man" (modern man), who consciously and voluntarily creates history, with the man of the traditional civilizations, who, as we have seen, had a negative attitude toward history. Whether he abolishes it periodically, whether he devaluates it by perpetually finding transhistorical models and archetypes for it, whether, finally, he gives it a metahistorical meaning (cyclical theory, eschatological significations, and so on), the man of the traditional civilizations accorded the historical event no value in itself; in other words, he did not regard it as a specific category of his own mode of existence. Now, to compare these two types of humanity implies an analysis of all the modern "historicisms," and such an analysis, to be really useful, would carry us too far from the principal theme of this study. We are nevertheless forced to touch upon the problem of man as consciously and voluntarily historical, because the modern world is, at the present moment, not entirely converted to historicism; we are even witnessing a conflict between the two views: the archaic conception, which we should designate as archetypal and anhistorical; and the

---

"The Terror of History" is the last essay in Eliade's widely read work, *The Myth of the Eternal Return*, published by Princeton University Press as part of the Bollinger Series (Princeton: 1954).

modern, post-Hegelian conception, which seeks to be historical. We shall confine ourselves to examining only one aspect of the problem, but an important aspect: the solutions offered by the historicistic view to enable modern man to tolerate the increasingly powerful pressure of contemporary history.

The foregoing chapters have abundantly illustrated the way in which men of the traditional civilizations tolerated history. The reader will remember that they defended themselves against it, either by periodically abolishing it through repetition of the cosmogony and a periodic regeneration of time or by giving historical events a metahistorical meaning, a meaning that was not only consoling but was above all coherent, that is, capable of being fitted into a well-consolidated system in which the cosmos and man's existence had each its *raison d'être*. We must add that this traditional conception of a defense against history, this way of tolerating historical events, continued to prevail in the world down to a time very close to our own; and that it still continues to console the agricultural (= traditional) societies of Europe, which obstinately adhere to an anhistorical position and are, by that fact, exposed to the violent attacks of all revolutionary ideologies. The Christianity of the popular European strata never succeeded in abolishing either the theory of the archetype (which transformed a historical personage into an exemplary hero and a historical event into a mythical category) or the cyclical and astral theories (according to which history was justified, and the sufferings provoked by it assumed an eschatological meaning). Thus—to give only a few examples—the barbarian invaders of the High Middle Ages were assimilated to the Biblical archetype Gog and Magog and thus received an ontological status and an eschatological function. A few centuries later, Christians were to regard Genghis Khan as a new David, destined to accomplish the prophecies of Ezekiel. Thus interpreted, the sufferings and catastrophes provoked by the appearance of the barbarians on the medieval historical horizon were "tolerated" by the same process that, some thousands of years earlier, had made it possible to tolerate the terrors of history in the ancient East. It is such justifications of historical catastrophes that today still make life possible for tens of millions of men, who continue to recognize, in the unremitting pressure of events, signs of the divine will or of an astral fatality.

If we turn to the other traditional conception—that of cyclical time and the periodic regeneration of history, whether or not it involves the myth of eternal repetition—we find that, although the earliest Christian writers began by violently opposing it, it nevertheless in the end made its way into Christian philosophy. We must remind ourselves that, for Christianity, time is real because it has a meaning—the Redemption. "A straight line traces the course of humanity from initial Fall to final

Redemption. And the meaning of this history is unique, because the Incarnation is a unique fact. Indeed, as Chapter 9 of the Epistle to the Hebrews and I Peter 3:18 emphasize, Christ died for our sins once only, once for all (*hapax, ephapax, semel*); it is not an event subject to repetition, which can be reproduced several times (*pollakis*). The development of history is thus governed and oriented by a unique fact, a fact that stands entirely alone. Consequently the destiny of all mankind, together with the individual destiny of each one of us, are both likewise played out once, once for all, in a concrete and irreplaceable time which is that of history and life."[1] It is this linear conception of time and history, which, already outlined in the second century by St. Irenaeus of Lyon, will be taken up again by St. Basil and St. Gregory and be finally elaborated by St. Augustine.

But despite the reaction of the orthodox Fathers, the theories of cycles and of astral influences on human destiny and historical events were accepted, at least in part, by other Fathers and ecclesiastical writers, such as Clement of Alexandria, Minucius Felix, Arnobius, and Theodoret. The conflict between these two fundamental conceptions of time and history continued into the seventeenth century. We cannot even consider recapitulating the admirable analyses made by Pierre Duhem and Lynn Thorndike, and resumed and completed by Pitirim Sorokin.[2] We must remind the reader that, at the height of the Middle Ages, cyclical and astral theories begin to dominate historiological and eschatological speculation. Already popular in the twelfth century,[3] they undergo systematic elaboration in the next, especially after the appearance of translations from Arabic writers.[4] Increasingly precise correlations are attempted between the cosmic and the geographical factors involved and the respective periodicities (in the direction already indicated by Ptolemy, in the second century of our era, in his *Tetrabiblos*). An Albertus Magnus, a St. Thomas, a Roger Bacon, a Dante (*Convivio*, II, Ch. 14), and many others believe that the cycles and periodicities of the world's history are governed by the influence of the stars, whether this influence obeys the will of God and is his instrument in history or whether—a hypothesis that gains increasing adherence—it is regarded as a force immanent in the cosmos.[5] In short, to adopt Sorokin's formulation, the Middle Ages are dominated by the eschatological conception (in its two essential moments: the creation and the end of the world), complemented by the theory of cyclic undulation that explains the periodic return of events. This twofold dogma dominates speculation down to the seventeenth century, although, at the same time, a theory of the linear progress of history begins to assert itself. In the Middle Ages, the germs of this theory can be recognized in the writings of Albertus Magnus and St. Thomas; but it is with the *Eternal Gospel* of Joachim of Floris that it appears in all its coherence, as an integral element of a magnificent eschatology of history, the most significant contribution of Christianity in this field since St. Augustine's. Joachim of Floris divides the history of the world into three great epochs, successively inspired and dominated by a different person of the Trinity: Father, Son, Holy Ghost. In the Calabrian abbot's vision, each of these epochs reveals, in history, a new dimension of the divinity and, by this fact, allows humanity to perfect itself progressively until finally, in the last phase—inspired by the Holy Ghost—it arrives at absolute spiritual freedom.[6]

But, as we said, the tendency which gains increasing adherence is that of an immanentization of the cyclical theory. Side by side with voluminous astrological treatises, the considerations of scientific astronomy assert themselves. So it is that in the theories of Tycho Brahe, Kepler, Cardano, Giordano Bruno, or Campanella, the cyclical ideology survives beside the new conception of linear progress professed, for example, by a Francis Bacon or a Pascal. From the seventeenth century on, linearism and the progressivistic conception of history assert themselves more and more, inaugurating faith in an infinite progress, a faith already proclaimed by Leibniz, predominant in the century of "enlightenment," and popularized in the nineteenth century by the triumph of the ideas of the evolutionists. We must wait until our own century to see the beginnings of certain new reactions against this historical linearism and a certain revival of interest in the theory of cycles;[7] so it is that, in political economy, we are witnessing the rehabilitation of the notions of cycle, fluctuation, periodic oscillation; that in philosophy the myth of eternal return is revivified by Nietzsche; or that, in the philosophy of history, a Spengler or a Toynbee concern themselves with the problem of periodicity.[8]

In connection with this rehabilitation of cyclical conceptions, Sorokin rightly observes[9] that present theories concerning the death of the universe do not exclude the hypothesis of the creation of a new universe, somewhat after the fashion of the Great Year in Greco-Oriental speculation or of the yuga cycle in the thought of India. Basically, it may be said that it is only in the cyclical theories of modern times that the meaning of the archaic myth of eternal repetition realizes its full implications. For the medieval cyclical theories confined themselves to justifying the periodicity of events by giving them an integral place in the rhythms of the cosmos and the fatalities of the stars. They thereby also implicitly affirmed the cyclical repetition of the events of history, even when this repetition was not regarded as continuing *ad infinitum*. Even more: by the fact that historical events depended upon cycles and astral situations, they became intelligible and even foreseeable, since they thus acquired a transcendent *model*; the wars, famines, and wretchedness provoked by contemporary history were at most only the repetition of an archetype, itself determined by the stars and by celestial norms from which the divine will was not always absent. As at the close of antiquity, these new expressions of the myth of eternal return were above all appreciated among the intellectual elites and especially consoled those who directly suffered the pressure of history. The peasant masses, in antiquity as in modern times, took less interest in cyclical and astral formulas; indeed, they found their consolation and support in the concept of archetypes and repetition, a concept that they "lived" less on the plane of the cosmos and the stars than on the mythico-historical level (transforming, for example, historical personages into exemplary heroes, historical events into mythical categories, and so on, in accordance with the dialectic which we defined above).

The Difficulties of Historicism

The reappearance of cyclical theories in contemporary thought is pregnant with meaning. Incompetent as we are to pass judgment upon their validity, we shall confine ourselves to observing that the formulation, in modern terms, of an archaic myth betrays at least the desire to find a meaning and a transhistorical justification for historical events. Thus we find ourselves once again in the pre-Hegelian position, the validity of the "historicistic" solutions, from Hegel to Marx, being implicitly called into question. From Hegel on, every effort is directed toward saving and conferring value on the historical event as such, the event in itself and for itself. In his study of the German Constitution, Hegel wrote that if we recognize that things are necessarily as they are, that is, that they are not arbitrary and not the result of chance, we shall at the same time recognize that they *must* be as they are. A century later, the concept of historical necessity will enjoy a more and more triumphant practical application: in fact, all the cruelties, aberrations, and tragedies of history have been, and still are, justified by the necessities of the "historical moment." Probably Hegel did not intend to go so far. But since he had resolved to reconcile himself with his own historical moment, he was obliged to see in every event the will of the Universal Spirit. This is why he considered "reading the morning papers a sort of realistic benediction of the morning." For him, only daily contact with events could orient man's conduct in his relations with the world and with God.

How could Hegel know what was *necessary* in history, what, consequently, must occur exactly as it had occurred? Hegel believed that he knew what the Universal Spirit wanted. We shall not insist upon the audacity of this thesis, which, after all, abolishes precisely what

Hegel wanted to save in history—human freedom. But there is an aspect of Hegel's philosophy of history that interests us because it still preserves something of the Judaeo-Christian conception: for Hegel, the historical event was the manifestation of the Universal Spirit. Now, it is possible to discern a parallel between Hegel's philosophy of history and the theology of history of the Hebrew prophets: for the latter, as for Hegel, an event is irreversible and valid in itself inasmuch as it is a new manifestation of the will of God—a proposition really revolutionary, we should remind ourselves, from the viewpoint of traditional societies dominated by the eternal repetition of archetypes. Thus, in Hegel's view, the destiny of a people still preserved a transhistorical significance, because all history revealed a new and more perfect manifestation of the Universal Spirit. But with Marx, history cast off all transcendental significance; it was no longer anything more than the epiphany of the class struggle. To what extent could such a theory justify historical sufferings? For the answer, we have but to turn to the pathetic resistance of a Belinsky or a Dostoevsky, for example, who asked themselves how, from the viewpoint of the Hegelian and Marxian dialectic, it was possible to redeem all the dramas of oppression, the collective sufferings, deportations, humiliations, and massacres that fill universal history.

Yet Marxism preserves a meaning to history. For Marxism, events are not a succession of arbitrary accidents; they exhibit a coherent structure and, above all, they lead to a definite end—final elimination of the terror of history, "salvation." Thus, at the end of the Marxist philosophy of history, lies the age of gold of the archaic eschatologies. In this sense it is correct to say not only that Marx "brought Hegel's philosophy back to earth" but also that he reconfirmed, upon an exclusively human level, the value of the primitive myth of the age of gold, with the difference that he puts the age of gold only at the end of history, instead of putting it at the beginning too. Here, for the militant Marxist, lies the secret of the remedy for the terror of history: just as the contemporaries of a "dark age" consoled themselves for their increasing sufferings by the thought that the aggravation of evil hastens final deliverance, so the militant Marxist of our day reads, in the drama provoked by the pressure of history, a necessary evil, the premonitory symptom of the approaching victory that will put an end forever to all historical "evil."

The terror of history becomes more and more intolerable from the viewpoints afforded by the various historicistic philosophies. For in them, of course, every historical event finds its full and only meaning in its realization alone. We need not here enter into the theoretical difficulties of historicism, which already troubled Rickert, Troeltsch, Dilthey, and Simmel, and which the recent efforts of Croce, of Karl Mannheim, or of Ortega y Gasset have but partially overcome.[10] This essay does not require us to discuss either the philosophical value of historicism as such or the possibility of establishing a "philosophy of history" that should definitely transcend relativism. Dilthey himself, at the age of seventy, recognized that "the relativity of all human concepts is the last word of the historical vision of the world." In vain did he proclaim an *allgemeine Lebenserfahrung* as the final means of transcending this relativity. In vain did Meinecke invoke "examination of conscience" as a transsubjective experience capable of transcending the relativity of historical life. Heidegger had gone to the trouble of showing that the historicity of human existence forbids all hope of transcending time and history.

For our purpose, only one question concerns us: How can the "terror of history" be tolerated from the viewpoint of historicism? Justification of a historical event by the simple fact that it is a historical event, in other words, by the simple fact that it "happened that way," will not go far toward freeing humanity from the terror that the event inspires. Be it understood that we are not here concerned with the problem of evil, which, from whatever angle it be viewed, remains a philosophical and religious problem; we are concerned with the problem of history as history, of the "evil" that is bound up not with man's condition but with his behavior toward others. We should wish to know, for example, how it would be possible to tolerate, and to justify, the sufferings and annihilation of so many peoples who suffer and are annihilated for the simple reason that their geographical situation sets them in the pathway of history; that they are neighbors of empires in a state of permanent expansion. How justify, for example, the fact that southeastern Europe had to suffer for centuries—and hence to renounce any impulse toward a higher historical existence, toward spiritual creation on the universal plane—for the sole reason that it happened to be on the road of the Asiatic invaders and later the neighbor of the Ottoman Empire? And in our day, when historical pressure no longer allows any escape, how can man tolerate the catastrophes and horrors of history—from collective deportations and massacres to atomic bombings—if beyond them he can glimpse no sign, no transhistorical meaning; if they are only the blind play of economic, social, or political forces, or, even worse, only the result of the "liberties" that a minority takes and exercises directly on the stage of universal history?

We know how, in the past, humanity has been able to endure the sufferings we have enumerated: they were regarded as a punishment inflicted by God, the syndrome of the decline of the "age," and so on. And it was possible to accept them precisely because they had a metahistorical meaning, because, for the greater part of mankind, still clinging to the traditional viewpoint, history did not have, and could not have, value in itself. Every hero repeated the archetypal gesture, every war rehearsed the struggle between good and evil, every fresh social injustice was identified with the sufferings of the Saviour (or, for example, in the pre-Christian world, with the passion of a divine messenger or vegetation god), each new massacre repeated the glorious end of the martyrs. It is not our part to decide whether such motives were puerile or not, or whether such a refusal of history always proved efficacious. In our opinion, only one fact counts: by virtue of this view, tens of millions of men were able, for century after century, to endure great historical pressures without despairing, without committing suicide or falling into that spiritual aridity that always brings with it a relativistic or nihilistic view of history.

Moreover, as we have already observed, a very considerable fraction of the population of Europe, to say nothing of the other continents, still lives today by the light of the traditional, anti-"historicistic" viewpoint. Hence it is above all the "elites" that are confronted with the problem, since they alone are forced, and with increasing rigor, to take cognizance of their historical situation. It is true that Christianity and the eschatological philosophy of history have not ceased to satisfy a considerable proportion of these elites. Up to a certain point, and for certain individuals, it may be said that Marxism—especially in its popular forms—represents a defense against the terror of history. Only the historicistic position, in all its varieties and shades—from Nietzsche's "destiny" to Heidegger's "temporality"—remains disarmed.[11] It is by no means mere fortuitous coincidence that, in this philosophy, despair, the *amor fati*, and pessimism are elevated to the rank of heroic virtues and instruments of cognition.

Yet this position, although the most modern and, in a certain sense, almost the inevitable position for all thinkers who define man as a "historical being," has not yet made a definitive conquest of contemporary thought. Some pages earlier, we noted various recent orientations that tend to reconfer value upon the myth of cyclical periodicity, even the myth of eternal return. These orientations disregard not only historicism but even history as such. We believe we are justified in seeing in them, rather than a resistance to history, a revolt against historical *time*, an attempt to restore this historical time, freighted as it is with human experience, to a place in the time that is cosmic, cyclical, and infinite. In any case it is worth noting that the work of two of the most significant writers of our day—T. S. Eliot and James Joyce—is saturated with nostalgia for the myth of eternal repetition and, in the last analysis, for the abolition of time. There is also reason to foresee that, as the terror of history grows worse, as existence becomes more and more precarious because of history, the positions of historicism will increasingly lose in prestige. And, at a moment when history could do what neither the cosmos, nor man, nor chance have yet succeeded in doing—that is, wipe out the human race in its entirety—it may be that we are witnessing a desperate attempt to prohibit the "events of history" through a reintegration of human societies within the horizon (artificial, because decreed) of archetypes and their repetition. In other words, it is not inadmissible to think of an epoch, and an epoch not too far distant, when humanity, to ensure its survival, will find itself reduced to desisting from any further "making" of history in the sense in which it began to make it from the creation of the first empires, will confine itself to repeating prescribed archetypal gestures, and will strive to forget, as meaningless and dangerous, any spontaneous gesture which might entail "historical" consequences. It would even be interesting to compare the an historical solution of future societies with the paradisal or eschatological myths of the golden age of the beginning or the end of the world. But as we have it in mind to pursue these speculations elsewhere, let us now return to our problem: the position of historical man in relation to archaic man, and let us attempt to understand the objections brought against the latter on the basis of the historicistic view.

Freedom and History

In his rejection of concepts of periodicity and hence, in the last analysis, of the archaic concepts of archetypes and repetition, we are, we believe, justified in seeing modern man's resistance to nature, the will of "historical man" to affirm his autonomy. As Hegel remarked, with noble self-assurance, nothing new ever occurs in nature. And the crucial difference between the man of the archaic civilizations and modern, historical man lies in the increasing value the latter gives to historical events, that is, to the "novelties" that, for traditional man, represented either meaningless conjunctures or infractions of norms (hence "faults," "sins," and so on) and that, as such, required to be expelled (abolished) periodically. The man who adopts the historical viewpoint would be justified in regarding the traditional conception of archetypes and repetition as an aberrant reidentification of history (that is, of "freedom" and "novelty") with nature (in which everything repeats itself). For, as modern man can observe, archetypes themselves constitute a "history" insofar as they are made up of gestures, acts, and decrees that, although supposed to have been manifested *in illo tempore*, were nevertheless manifested, that is, came to birth in time, "took place," like any other historical event. Primitive myths often mention the birth, activity, and disappearance of a god or a hero whose "civilizing" gestures are thenceforth repeated *ad infinitum*. This comes down to saying that archaic man also knows a history, although it is a primordial history, placed in a mythical time. Archaic man's rejection of history, his refusal to situate himself in a concrete, historical time, would, then, be the symptom of a precocious weariness, a fear of movement and spontaneity; in short, placed between accepting the historical condition and its risks on the one hand, and his reidentification with the modes of nature on the other, he would choose such a reidentification.

In this total adherence, on the part of archaic man, to archetypes and repetition, modern man would be justified in seeing not only the primitives' amazement at their own first spontaneous and creative free gestures and their veneration, repeated *ad infinitum*, but also a feeling of guilt on the part of man hardly emerged from the paradise of animality (i.e., from nature), a feeling that urges him to reidentify with nature's eternal repetition the few primordial, creative, and spontaneous gestures that had signalized the appearance of freedom. Continuing his critique, modern man could even read in this fear, this hesitation or fatigue in the presence of any gesture without an archetype, nature's tendency toward equilibrium and rest; and he would read this tendency in the anticlimax that fatally follows upon any exuberant gesture of life and that some have gone so far as to recognize in the need felt by human reason to unify the real through knowledge. In the last analysis, modern man, who accepts history or claims to accept it, can reproach archaic man, imprisoned within the mythical horizon of archetypes and repetition, with his creative impotence, or, what amounts to the same thing, his inability to accept the risks entailed by every creative act. For the modern man can be creative only insofar as he is historical; in other words, all creation is forbidden him except that which has its source in his own freedom; and, consequently, everything is denied him except the freedom to make history by making himself.

To these criticisms raised by modern man, the man of the traditional civilizations could reply by a countercriticism that would at the same time be a defense of the type of archaic existence. It is becoming more and more doubtful, he might say, if modern man can make history. On the contrary, the more modern[12] he becomes—that is, without defenses against the terror of history—the less chance he has of himself making history. For history either makes itself (as the result of the seed sown by acts that occurred in the past, several centuries or even several millennia ago; we will cite the consequences of the discovery of agriculture or metallurgy, of the Industrial Revolution in the eighteenth century, and so on) or it tends to be made by an increasingly smaller number of men who not only prohibit the mass of their contemporaries from directly or indirectly intervening in the history they are making (or which the small group is making), but in addition have at their disposal means sufficient to force each individual to endure, for his own part, the consequences of this history, that is, to live immediately and continuously in dread of history. Modern man's boasted freedom to make history is illusory for nearly the whole of the human race. At most, man is left free to choose between two positions: (1) to oppose the history that is being made by the very small minority (and, in this case, he is free to choose between suicide and deportation); (2) to take refuge in a subhuman existence or in flight. The "freedom" that historical existence implies was possible—and even then within certain limits—at the beginning of the modern period, but it tends to become inaccessible as the period becomes more historical, by which we mean more alien from any transhistorical model. It is perfectly natural, for example, that Marxism and Fascism must lead to the establishment of two types of historical existence: that of the leader (the only really "free" man) and that of the followers, who find, in the historical existence of the leader, not an archetype of their own existence but the lawgiver of the gestures that are provisionally permitted them.

Thus, for traditional man, modern man affords the type neither of a free being nor of a creator of history. On the contrary, the man of the archaic civilizations can be proud of his mode of existence, which allows him to be free and to create. He is free to be no longer what he was, free to annul his own history through periodic abolition of time and collective regeneration. This freedom in respect to his own history—which, for the modern, is not only irreversible but constitutes human existence—cannot be claimed by the man who wills to be historical. We know that the archaic and traditional societies granted freedom each year to begin a new, a "pure" existence, with virgin possibilities. And there is no question of seeing in this an imitation of nature, which also undergoes periodic regeneration, "beginning anew" each spring, with each spring recovering all its powers intact. Indeed, whereas nature repeats itself, each new spring being the same eternal spring (that is, the repetition of the Creation), archaic man's "purity" after the periodic abolition of time and the recovery of his virtualities intact allows him, on the threshold of each "new life," a continued existence in eternity and hence the definitive abolition, *hic et nunc*, of profane time. The intact "possibilities" of nature each spring and archaic man's possibilities on the threshold of each year are, then, not homologous. Nature recovers only itself, whereas archaic man recovers the possibility of definitively transcending time and living in eternity. Insofar as he fails to do so, insofar as he "sins," that is, falls into historical existence, into time, he each year thwarts the possibility. At least he retains the freedom to annul his faults, to wipe out the memory of his "fall into history," and to make another attempt to escape definitively from time.[13]

Furthermore, archaic man certainly has the right to consider himself more creative than modern man, who sees himself as creative only in respect to history. Every year, that is, archaic man takes part in the repetition of the cosmogony, the creative act par excellence. We may even add that, for a certain time, man was creative on the cosmic plane, imitating this periodic cosmogony (which he also repeated on all the other planes of life) and participating in it.[14] We should also bear in mind the "creationistic" implications of the Oriental philosophies and techniques (especially the Indian), which thus find a place in the same traditional horizon. The East unanimously rejects the idea of the ontological irreducibility of the existent, even though it too sets out from a sort of "existentialism" (i.e., from acknowledging suffering as the situation of any possible cosmic condition). Only, the East does not accept the destiny of the human being as final and irreducible. Oriental techniques attempt above all to annul or transcend the human condition. In this respect, it is justifiable to speak not only of freedom (in the positive sense) or deliverance (in the negative sense) but actually of creation; for what is involved is creating a new man and creating him on a suprahuman plane, a man-god, such as the imagination of historical man has never dreamed it possible to create.

Despair or Faith

However this may be, our dialogue between archaic man and modern man does not affect our problem. Whatever be the truth in respect to the freedom and the creative virtualities of historical man, it is certain that none of the historicistic philosophies is able to defend him from the terror of history. We could even imagine a final attempt: to save history and establish an ontology of history, events would be regarded as a series of "situations" by virtue of which the human spirit should attain knowledge of levels of reality otherwise inaccessible to it. This attempt to justify history is not without interest,[15] and we anticipate returning to the subject elsewhere. But we are able to observe here and now that such a position affords a shelter from the terror of history only insofar as it postulates the existence at least of the Universal Spirit. What consolation should we find in knowing that the sufferings of millions of men have made possible the revelation of a limitary situation of the human condition if, beyond that limitary situation, there should be only nothingness? Again, there is no question here of judging the validity of a historicistic philosophy, but only of establishing to what extent such a philosophy can exorcise the terror of history. If, for historical tragedies to be excused, it suffices that they should be regarded as the means by which man has been enabled to know the limit of human resistance, such an excuse can in no way make man less haunted by the terror of history.

Basically, the horizon of archetypes and repetition cannot be transcended with impunity unless we accept a philosophy of freedom that does not exclude God. And indeed this proved to be true when the horizon of archetypes and repetition was transcended, for the first time, by Judaeo-Christianism, which introduced a new category into religious experience: the category of *faith*. It must not be forgotten that, if Abraham's faith can be defined as "for God everything is possible," the faith of Christianity implies that everything is also possible for man. ". . . Have faith in God. For verily I say unto you, That whosoever shall say unto this mountain, Be thou removed, and be thou cast into the sea; and shall not doubt in his heart, but shall believe that those things which he saith shall come to pass; he shall have whatsoever he saith. Therefore I say unto you, What things soever ye desire, when ye pray, believe that ye receive them, and ye shall have them" (Mark 11:22–24).[16] Faith, in this context, as in many others, means absolute emancipation from any kind of natural "law" and hence the highest freedom that man can imagine: freedom to intervene even in the ontological constitution of the universe. It is, consequently, a pre-eminently creative freedom. In other words, it constitutes a new formula for man's collaboration with the creation—the first, but also the only such formula accorded to him since the traditional horizon of archetypes and repetition was transcended. Only such a freedom (aside from its soteriological, hence, in the strict sense, its religious value) is able to defend modern man from the terror of history—a freedom, that is, which has its source and finds its guaranty and support in God. Every other modern freedom, whatever satisfactions it may procure to him who possesses it, is powerless to justify history; and this, for every man who is sincere with himself, is equivalent to the terror of history.

We may say, furthermore, that Christianity is the "religion" of modern man and historical man, of the man who simultaneously discovered personal freedom and continuous time (in place of cyclical time). It is even interesting to note that the existence of God forced itself far more urgently upon modern man, for whom history exists as such, as history and not as repetition, than upon the man of the archaic and traditional cultures, who, to defend himself from the terror of history, had at his disposition all the myths, rites, and customs mentioned in the course of this book. Moreover, although the idea of God and the religious experiences that it implies existed from the most distant ages, they could be, and were, replaced at times by other religious "forms" (totemism, cult of ancestors, Great Goddesses of fecundity, and so on) that more promptly answered the religious needs of primitive humanity. In the horizon of archetypes and repetition, the terror of history, when it appeared, could be supported. Since the "invention" of faith, in the Judaeo-Christian sense of the word (= for God all is possible), the man who has left the horizon of archetypes and repetition can no longer defend himself against that terror except through the idea of God. In fact, it is only by presupposing the existence of God that he conquers, on the one hand, freedom (which grants him autonomy in a universe governed by laws or, in other words, the "inauguration" of a mode of being that is new and unique in the universe) and, on the other hand, the certainty that historical tragedies have a transhistorical meaning, even if that meaning is not always visible for humanity in its present condition. Any other situation of modern man leads, in the end, to despair. It is a despair provoked not by his own human existentiality, but by his presence in a historical universe in which almost the whole of mankind lives prey to a continual terror (even if not always conscious of it).

In this respect, Christianity incontestibly proves to be the religion of "fallen man": and this to the extent to which modern man is irremediably identified with history and progress, and to which history and progress are a fall, both implying the final abandonment of the paradise of archetypes and repetition.

Notes

1. Henri-Charles Puech, "Gnosis and Time," in *Man and Time* (New York and London: 1957), pp. 48ff. Cf. also the same author's "Temps, histoire et mythe dans le christianisme des premiers siècles," *Proceedings of the VIIth Congress for the History of Religion* (Amsterdam: 1951), pp. 33–52.

2. Pierre Duhem, *Le Systeme du monde* (Paris: 1913–1917); Lynne Thorndike, *A History of Magic and Experimental Science* (New York: 1929–1941); Pitirim A. Sorokin, *Social and Cultural Dynamics*, II (New York: 1937–1941).

3. Thorndike, I, pp. 455ff; Sorokin, p. 371.

4. Duhem, V, pp. 223ff.

5. Ibid., pp. 225ff.; Thorndike, II, pp. 267ff., 416ff., etc.; Sorokin, p. 371.

6. It was a real tragedy for the Western world that Joachim of Floris' prophetico-eschatological speculations, though they inspired and fertilized the thought of a St. Francis of Assisi, of a Dante, and of a Savonarola, so quickly sank into oblivion, the Calabrian monk surviving only as a name to which could be attached a multitude of apocryphal writings. The imminence of spiritual freedom, not only in respect to dogma but also in respect to society (a freedom that Joachim conceived as a necessity of both divine and historical dialectics), was again professed, at a later period, by the ideologies of the Reformation and the

Renaissance, but in entirely different terms and in accordance with different spiritual views.

7. Sorokin, pp. 379ff.

8. Cf. A. Rey, *Le Retour eternel et la philosophie de la physique* (Paris: 1927); Pitirim A. Sorokin, *Contemporary Sociological Theories* (New York: 1928), pp. 728–741; Arnold J. Toynbee, *A Study of History, III* (London: 1934); Ellsworth Huntinton, *Mainsprings of Civilization* (New York: 1945), especially pp. 453 ff.; Jean Claude Antoine, "L'Eternel Retour de l'histoire deviendra-t-il objet de science?" *Critique* XXVII (August, 1948):723ff.

9. Sorokin, p. 383, n80.

10. Let us say, first of all, that the terms "historicism" and "historism" cover many different and antagonistic philosophical currents and orientations. It is enough to recall Dilthey's vitalistic relativism, Croce's "storicismo," Gentile's "attualismo," and Ortega's "historical reason" to realize the multiplicity of philosophical valuations accorded to history during the first half of the twentieth century. For Croce's present position, see his *La storia come pensiero e come azione* (Bari: 1938; 7th rev. ed., 1965); also, J. Ortega y Gasset, *Historia como sistema* (Madrid: 1941); Karl Mannheim, *Ideology and Utopia*, trans. by Louis Wirth and Edward Shils (New York: 1936). On the problem of history, see also Pedro Lain Entralgo, *Medicina e historia* (Madrid: 1941); and Karl Lowith, *Meaning in History* (Chicago: 1949).

11. We take the liberty of emphasizing that "historicism" was created and professed above all by thinkers belonging to nations for which history has never been a continuous terror. These thinkers would perhaps have adopted another viewpoint had they belonged to nations marked by the "fatality of history." It would certainly be interesting, in any case, to know if the theory according to which everything that happens is "good," simply because it has happened, would have been accepted without qualms by the thinkers of the Baltic countries, of the Balkans, or of colonial territories.

12. It is well to make clear that, in this context, "modern man" is such in his insistence upon being exclusively historical; i.e., that he is, above all, the "man" of historicism, of Marxism, and of existentialism. It is superfluous to add that not all of our contemporaries recognize themselves in such a man.

13. On this, see our *Patterns in Comparative Religion*, English translation (London and New York: 1958), pp. 398ff.

14. Not to mention the possibilities of "magical creation" which exist in traditional societies and which are real.

15. It is only through some such reasoning that it would be possible to found a sociology of knowledge that should not lead to relativism and skepticism. The "influences"—economic, social, national, cultural—that affect "ideologies" (in the sense which Karl Mannheim gave the term) would not annul their objective value any more than the fever or the intoxication that reveals to a poet a new poetic creation would impair the value of the latter. All these social, economic, and other influences would, on the contrary, be occasions for envisaging a spiritual universe from new angles. But it goes without saying that a sociology

of knowledge, that is, the study of the social conditioning of ideologies, could avoid relativism only by affirming the autonomy of the spirit—which, if we understand him aright, Karl Mannheim did not dare to affirm.

16. Such affirmations must not be complacently dismissed merely because they imply the possibility of miracle. If miracles have been so rare since the appearance of Christianity, the blame rests not on Christianity but on Christians.

The Criterion Group:
From Freud
to Charlie Chaplin

This excerpt from Autobiography: Volume I, 1907–1937, Journey East, Journey West *recounts Eliade's intense involvement in the Criterion symposia as a young intellectual in Romania.*

I believe it was I who inaugurated the cycle on Freud. Among other speakers for that symposium I remember only Mircea Vulcănescu and Paul Sterian, but there were five or six of us, including a psychoanalyst. When I entered the hall I could hardly believe my eyes. The auditorium was full and overflowing. Seats on the main floor had been sold out well in advance, and people were crowded into the balcony and galleries. They sat wherever they could: on the stairs, on the railings. And then, because no one could hold them back, they had pushed into the main auditorium and were leaning against the walls and even sitting on the stage. Likely we should not have been able to begin if Petru Comarnescu had not announced in the auditorium and foyer that we would repeat the symposium a few days later, and that with the cooperation of the fire department we would close and bolt the entryway door.

I had agreed to speak about Freud because I thought I could decipher in his work a final phase in the desacralization of Old Testament monotheism and propheticism. Freud's certainty that he had found a unique and universal meaning for psychomental life and human creativity,

From *Autobiography: Volume I: 1907–1937, Journey East, Journey West*, 232–237. Reprinted with permission of Harper and Row and the author.

that he had forged the magic key that would unlock all enigmas from dreams and *actes manqués* to the origin of religion, morals, and civilization—this certainty, I said, betrayed the monotheistic fervor of the Hebraic genius. In the same way, the passion expended by Freud in promoting, imposing, and defending psychoanalysis from any "heresy" is reminiscent of the intolerance and frenzy of Old Testament prophets. In a certain sense, Freud believed that his discoveries were destined to transform mankind, to "save" it. Psychoanalysis satisfied the thirst for the absolute, characteristic of the Judaic genius, the belief that there is a *single* royal road to the Spirit, and it betrays the specifically Hebraic revulsion toward pluralism, polytheism, and idolatry.

I don't know how clearly and articulately I said these things that evening. Like the other participants, I was rewarded with loud, prolonged applause. I learned later that Emil Cioran had been so impressed that he had come to hear us the second time when we repeated the symposium. (We repeated it twice, and then we gave it I don't know how many times in provincial cities.)

The other symposia followed, two per week, with equal success. A half hour ahead of time the auditorium of the King Carol I Foundation would be full to the last seat, and the participants would have difficulty making their way through the crowds gathered on the sidewalk. With great effort, assisted by the police, they would gain entrance to the crowded foyer. The municipal police had found it necessary to send a dozen sergeants and several captains to ensure traffic circulation in front of the Foundation, and to defend the entrances from the throng. This unprecedented success disturbed the Minister of the Interior, irritated a goodly number of journalists and writers, and gave rise to all sorts of envy and jealousy. And of course our risks increased as the personalities we discussed became more controversial. Just as we feared, the symposium on Gide gave rise to incidents. André Gide had visited Soviet Russia a short while before and was considered a Communist. That evening about a hundred nationalist students tried to gain entry to the auditorium. Halted by the police, they began to sing and raise a clamor. The symposium began, but the hall was charged with electricity. Several of our group went outside to talk with the head of the demonstrators. They parleyed for better than an hour. The students claimed they had not come to provoke a disturbance, but only to listen, to be sure that no apology for communism was made. Finally, we let them inside. The symposium came to an end soon afterward, but I do not think it ended that evening as it had been planned. Shortly after being admitted into the crowded hall the students began shouting, and the moderator closed the session with a few ironic, sarcastic remarks that were lost in the tumult.

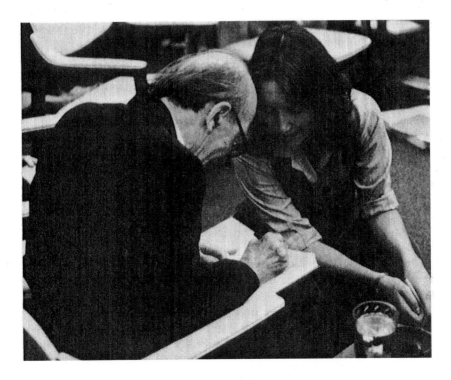

A less serious incident, and one that ended in our favor, occurred at the symposium on Charlie Chaplin. Among the speakers was Mihail Sebastian. When his turn came, someone shouted from the gallery: "One Jew talking about another Jew!" Mihail was on his feet, holding several sheets of paper on which he had written an outline of his remarks. He became very pale. Tearing up his notes, he took a step forward and began to speak in a voice choked with emotion. "I had planned to speak about a certain aspect of Chaplin's acting," he said, "but someone out there has called attention to our Jewishness. So I shall speak as a Jew about the Jew, Charlie Chaplin."

Suddenly the audience burst into applause. Mihail Sebastian raised his arm. "Thank you!" he said, and then he improvised one of the most moving and intelligent lectures I have ever had the opportunity to hear. He presented a Chaplin whom only someone from Eastern Europe could imagine and understand. He spoke about the loneliness of man in Chaplin's films as a reflection of the loneliness of the ghetto. When he finished speaking twenty minutes later, he was rewarded with a tremendously enthusiastic ovation. Part of the audience rose to its feet. We had won a battle, and we knew it. In the office that connected with the speaker's box, there was exultation. For joy, Nina Mareş began to dance and hug us one after another.

For the symposium on Lenin, we invited both Belu Silber and Lucreţiu Pătrăşcanu to take part. We wanted to have two Marxists to participate along with Mircea Vulcănescu and Mihail Polihronaide, who were prepared to criticize communism in the name of democracy and nationalism. Belu Silber I had met some time before at the editorial office of *Cuvântul*. He and Racoveanu had been friends ever since the latter had written an article in his defense when he was on trial two years earlier, accused of espionage. Belu Silber had been moved greatly by the article and immediately after his acquittal he had come to thank Racoveanu. From then on he visited the editorial office rather frequently. He became good friends especially with Mircea Vulcănescu, Ion Călugăru, and Paul Sterian. Small in stature, Silber was a brilliant, well-educated man, and although he repeated constantly that he was a Marxist, he seemed neither dogmatic nor intolerant. He admired me in particular because in my articles on India I attacked colonialism and the British Raj.

Lucreţiu Pătrăşcanu I met only that evening, I believe. I liked his face, which was kind and at the same time grave. He spoke without éclat, but sincerely and with a wise sobriety. Interruptions by students in the audience didn't bother him. He waited until the uproar died down, and then he took up his exposition again, calmly and intently. In contrast, the students interrupted Polihroniade with applause every time he spoke of the necessity of a nationalistic revolution. And when he referred to the expression of Lenin's that the bourgeois state is a cadaver that will topple at a single blow, he was applauded as much by the nationalistic students as by the groups of Communist sympathizers who had been drawn to the Foundation by the scheduled appearance of Pătrăşcanu.

Following this symposium the rumor was spread, especially among the security forces, that the Criterion group was crypto-Communistic. The truth was that the only Communist among us was Belu Silber. But the audacity we had shown in inviting the secretary of the Communist Party himself to speak at the Carol I Foundation had been misconstrued. We had tried to be "objective": *audiatur et altera pars*. We said that, in a major culture, all currents of thought can be presented. We felt strong enough not to be afraid of confrontations with ideologies and systems contrary to our own beliefs. Likewise, we felt that we could not get beyond cultural provincialism except by annulling the inferiority complexes and infantile defense mechanisms inherent in any minor culture. Having come to believe in the creative possibilities of the Romanian genius—as the majority of us did, although for different reasons—we no longer feared "evil influences" or "subversive ideas." On the other hand, we considered ourselves adults; we were unwilling to have people shout at us, "Don't play with fire!"—because we knew very well that we were not playing.

That which was later called the "spirit of Criterion" became clearer and more articulate the longer the program ran. But even from the first few symposia, the public discerned that this was a significant cultural experiment and one of great proportions—and they remained faithful to us until the end. Even when the subject was not a sensational one like Lenin, Freud, or Gide, the auditorium was full. In the symposium about the contemporary Romanian novel, Mihail Sebastian executed Cezar Petrescu *con molto brio,* and he was extremely hard on Ionel Teodoreanu, the most popular novelist of the day—reserving all his plaudits for Hortensia Papadat-Bengescu, Camil Petrescu, and Matei Caragiale. But Vulcănescu showed in what sense Cezar Petrescu's novels are integrated into a Romanian literary tradition and are significant even if they are not artistically valuable. What excited the enthusiasm of the audience was the dialogue between members of the Criterion group. Very seldom, and only in the case of sensitive subjects—for instance, Lenin and Mussolini—did the speakers get together beforehand and make rigorous preparations for the symposium. Ordinarily, each one would announce the observations he had in mind to develop. Only if we saw that two or more of the participants intended to make the same points did we ask them to modify their plans. In any event, the spontaneity of the dialogue was almost always assured. This gave rise, at times, to amusing scenes. For instance, when we discussed America vis-à-vis Europe and the Far East, Comarnescu, who identified himself to some extent with the American man and American culture, endured rather calmly the criticisms I made in the name of Oriental spirituality, but he lost his temper with Sebastian derided *Homo Americanus* in the name of the French spirit, and he tried to interrupt him several times during his presentation. Even after being called to order by the moderator, he continued to shout, to guffaw, or to turn his back abruptly in his chair every time he thought Sebastian went too far.

*   *   *

For the members of Criterion, the symposium did not end in the auditorium of the Foundation. We all gathered at the Cafe Corso, where we occupied a whole corner of the second floor and continued our discussion until after midnight. Usually Dan Botta, who rarely took part in the symposia, expressed his opinions then, succinctly and mercilessly. He never forgot to remind us of the responsibility we had toward the public. For him, this meant above all the duty to lift the public, not up to our level, but beyond, to our *ideals*. Dan believed that Criterion could effect, in the minds of the more intelligent members of the audience, an operation of Platonic *anamnesis*. In attending our symposia, where many points of view were presented and debated, the public actually was witnessing a new type of Socratic dialogue. The goal we were pursuing was not only to inform people; above all, we were seeking to "awaken" the audience, to confront them with ideas, and ultimately to modify their mode of being in the world.

Of course there ensued long, animated discussions. Not because the others did not share Dan's ideas about the role of Criterion, but because they were not always in accord with the methods he advocated. Botta insisted that at least one of the participants ought not to make any concessions to the average listener, but instead ought to use the technical vocabulary of metaphysics, science, poetry, or whatever the subject might be. Usually it happened that way anyhow. But as some of us saw it, the very fact that we were debating difficult problems was courageous enough without aggravating the difficulty by employing excessively technical language. But of course we were all agreed that every speaker was free to use whatever style he pleased.

————§§————

Encounter
and Reflection:
Essays by
Seminar Participants

ROBERT A. POIS

—————§§—————

Sacred Space, Historicity, and Mircea Eliade

In the fall of 1976, my wife Anne Marie and I, after spending some months in Germany where I was engaged in research projects, travelled extensively in Eastern Europe. Research projects, particularly in Poland, were partly the reason for this, but in fact the visit was due mostly to curiosity. To me Eastern Europe was that unfamiliar, vaguely disquieting "other," a place both burdened and illuminated by tragedy. From what we knew of it—mainly through history books and music—it offered a striated pattern of gray vistas with outbursts of local color. Also, of particular interest to me as a railroad "buff," it offered steam locomotives, with luck, perhaps in large numbers.

There was another angle to it, particularly for me as a Jew, and that was the ineradicable fact that Eastern Europe had been the graveyard of European Jewry. Chassidism had been born in the wake of the Chmelnitskii bloodbath and been nurtured there and spread throughout the region. Zionism, although in a large measure the result of Central European intellectual musings, received most of its spiritual support in Eastern Europe as did its antipode, the Jewish Bundist movement. Everything, of course, had been swept away, and all that was left were monuments erected and preserved by regimes that, officially tolerant and anti-Zionist (somehow the two were supposed to be seen as going together), have been ideologically compelled to understate World War II slaughters as specifically involving Jews. Nazi massacres had been augmented by a conscientious assault on historical memory.

From time to time, it occurred to me that, particularly since neither of us spoke any Eastern European language—we relied on German, English, a little French, and a few Russian words to see us through—and our "intellectual" involvements in Eastern Europe were thus relatively limited, an overwhelming emotional revulsion should have prevented me from visiting such a place, local color or no. Indeed, Anne Marie, whose sensitivity to historical issues is at least as acute as mine, occasionally raised this point, and not only because she found places such as Warsaw (which was experiencing the coldest early fall in recent memory) quite uncongenial. She shared my awareness that many of the Eastern European populations hated Jews in a far more personal and thus intense fashion than did those Germans who planned and carried out the "Final Solution." Moreover, we shared the knowledge that, while there were few Jews left in Eastern Europe, there was still no lack of hatred of them—a hatred as genuine and "folksy" as horse-drawn carts or liquor-fueled cafe sentimentalities.

To be sure, there was much genuine historical interest to be seen— although in many places the ravages of the Turks, who seemed to have their own concepts of urban renewal, obviated the possibility of seeing much put together before the sixteenth century—but, why spend so much time here? After all, these were police states and, with the exceptions of Hungary and Yugoslavia, this was almost everywhere apparent. In this regard, I at least experienced an initial fascination with jack-boots, submachine guns, and heavily guarded frontiers. But even this downright pathological interest on my part could last for only a limited amount of time. Once the initial "thrill" of encountering the impediments of authoritarianism wore off, I found myself to be alternately bored or frightened by it. When, sometime in November we eventually left Eastern Europe, quite possibly for good, we felt a vague sense of relief. Also, as a student of history, I found this to be particularly distressing: neither of us thought that our historical appreciation of the region had been increased very much. Things had turned out to be different from what we had expected—some things worse, some things better—but on the whole, except for idiosyncratic encounters of one sort or another, our appreciation of the place was about what it would have been had we never been there. Throughout the trip the food was better than anticipated, there was appreciably more gray than color—though this might have been due to the season—and while steam engines were visible in fairly large numbers few, alas, were "main-line." Upon our return to the States, I found myself trying to figure out ("pondering" would be much too profound a word to describe it) what the Eastern Europe adventure meant. For, despite the various caveats mentioned, it obviously had meant *something*. Yet, the usual categories of explanation seemed not to apply.

Of course events and issues of a far more crucial nature supervened. Anne Marie, during a stay in Los Angeles, came to play an important role in the Judy Chicago Project, a vital effort to utilize art in the service of women's history. In September 1978, Emily was born, and besides the usual travails, brought joy into our lives and into that of my mother (whose death in May 1981 has yet to be fully assimilated). Although never in any particularly dramatic way, the trip to Eastern Europe, or rather the meaning of it, continued to preoccupy me. Furthermore, important events, such as those I've mentioned, had the uncanny, unsettling effect of not bringing the issue into sharper focus, but rather lengthening the shadow it occasionally seemed to cast across my feelings and perceptions. There was an inarticulated singularity about it.

In the spring of 1982 my colleague the distinguished historian of Latin America, William B. Taylor, told me that a highly respected friend of his, Davíd Carrasco, was organizing a seminar concerned with the life and work of Mircea Eliade, who would be visiting the campus in the fall of that year. Bill knew of my interest in ideology as secular religion and political symbolism. Could he tell Davíd that I was interested in participating in this seminar? Naturally I was flattered; yet, from what I knew of Professor Eliade's work, I was also a bit troubled. Of course, like quite a few of my colleagues, I was familiar with at least some of his writings, certainly enough of them to appreciate why he was generally viewed as one of the leading historians of religion of this century.

One of Professor Eliade's primary concerns, the continued role of religion (or at least the religious experience) in an increasingly secular world, was also a concern of mine. It was here that difficulties intruded, centering around what I perceived to be a major difference between Professor Eliade's attitude toward the role of religion or "mysticism" in day-to-day life and my own. In short, he seemed to be positively disposed toward that intimate connection, and I was—and am—not. Although not a Marxist, I have always believed in Wilhelm Reich's assertion that the role of mysticism in a secular setting has necessarily been reactionary. Fascism in general, and National Socialism in particular, was (in fact, had to be) the political expression of seemingly nontranscendental efforts to sanctify the mundane. As a student of history, I thought that there was a very strong antihistorical bias at work in this. Political mysticism seemed to involve a sort of stepping out of history, a flight from that historicity which stamps the race as human. One of the criticisms of Eliade's approach to the history of religion with which I was familiar was that it was antihistorical through and through, and after a quick looking back upon what I knew of his work, I tended to agree with this. For me, a somewhat more immediately sobering thought came to the fore, that Professor Eliade's concern with the sanctification of mundane life could well have led to a more specific concern with the sanctification of *national* life. Romanian history, particularly since World War I, offered several examples of this, the Iron Guard perhaps

being the most spectacular. What I found myself thinking was, what did Eliade have to do with all that? Yet, even as these troubling considerations nagged at me, the awesome expanse of the man's knowledge (as well as his extraordinary and perhaps, in his field, unequalled, syncretic abilities) enthralled me. Knowing that I might feel quite out of place, I nonetheless joined the Eliade seminar with enthusiasm.

Previously, I had always considered religion in relation to something else. The Judaeo-Christian view of history (heroically unilinear instead of being cyclical) had provided a crucial underpinning for my historiography class. Religion as a source of artistic inspiration had been of particular concern and this had served to deepen my interest in one of the great "modern" painters who often dealt with religious themes, Emil Nolde. Religious justifications for and arguments against war were a perennial as, I suspect, they are for most of those who have ever concerned themselves with the history of ideas. The religious basis of German Idealism, and thus necessarily Marxism (another "perennial"), was an issue that seemed never to lose its power to fascinate. Finally, as I've mentioned earlier, the role of religion in secularized garb, i.e., as ideology, a far more disturbing theme (for me), served to color not merely my approach to Eliade and the seminar, but also my approach to the political and the world of ideas in general.

In the seminar (often, it seemed, against my will) I found myself considering religious issues per se, something that I could not remember having done since preparing for my Bar Mitzvah (an affair which in retrospect, had served to call into question the pertinence of religious values in the everyday life of at least one alienated twelve- to thirteen-year-old boy). As we considered various of Eliade's writings, I kept waiting for one or the other of the seminar members to bring in political philosophy or some canon of aesthetic experience to make the whole thing "relevant." Occasionally this happened, and more often than not, I was the participant who did this. Yet while the seminar members certainly seemed to be interested in my efforts to add dimensions of historical verisimilitude to the experience, I got the impression that somehow I was missing the point. Gradually it sank in that despite the fact that I was only one of several participants who was not in the field of comparative religion or the history of religion, this was indeed a seminar whose primary focus *had* to be varieties of religious experience as these had been filtered through and syncretized by one of the sovereign minds in religious studies.

As we considered various works, particularly *Patterns in Comparative Religion,* it became even more obvious than before that Professor Eliade's focus upon the forms of religious experience in themselves (in its rejection, or at least oversight, of putative developmental patterns) could be seen as antihistorical. If one turned to the very general use of "Historicism" (of which Karl Popper is the best example), one could rapidly conclude that Eliade was on the side of those who thought that the inherently teleological nature of historical thinking contained within it elements that were fundamentally inimical to understanding religious experience. This conclusion seemed particularly apt when one considered the notion of "sacred" versus "profane" time, the historiographical consequences of which seemed to be pretty well sketched out in *The Myth of the Eternal Return.* It seemed to me that Professor Eliade's approach was indeed so antihistorical that, from time to time, I wondered why he wanted to be known as a "historian of religion." If one bore in mind Croce's vital distinction between history (as something alive and relevant), and chronicle (sort of the phenomenal raw material of the historical imagination), Eliade's involvement with past issues seemed to be that of a chronicler. Past data existed to confirm the persistence of universal efforts to delineate a sacred realm immune to the vulgar (i.e., profane) time that, in its protean nature, constitutes both the realm and object of historical investigation.

Yet, as the seminar continued to meet, I found myself again and again coming back to the term "Historicism," not as used by Karl Popper, but in the perhaps narrower sense in which it has been seen as characterizing a peculiarly German method of historical investigation. Historicism, which (depending on how one looked at it) began either with the cultural investigations of Johann Gottfried Herder or with the putatively self-confident statism of Leopold von Ranke, represented history in its most self-assured mode. Certainly (at least for Ranke, and those who followed him), there was expressed a confidence in history as being inherently self-justifying that even Hegel had not exhibited. The historical mind was seen as being intuitively and ineluctably drawn to objects of investigation that (due to the very fact that they *were* such objects) represented concrete embodiments of universal truths. At issue here was an approach that emphasized the so-called "historical individuality," in short, any past phenomenon, be it a state, state institution, "age," or cultural artifact that, for reasons initially empathetic, attracted the purview of the historical imagination and hence was an object of historical investigation. The historical quest, focused as it was upon individualities infused with universal values, was, in and of itself, meaningful and the knowledge thus derived *ultimately* so. With regards to the question of Mircea Eliade *contra* history, so far, so bad. Historicism at high tide testified to the sacred nature of historical time; in fact, so far as any sort of meaning was concerned, *non*historical time would appear to have been a contradiction in terms. Yet the historicist angle kept gnawing at me, and gradually I came to realize that I was being drawn to reflecting upon one who in many ways, has come to represent the thinking of Historicism at "low tide," Friedrich Meinecke.

World War I, particularly Germany's defeat in it, had caused Meinecke to back away from that positivizing of history, particularly that of its statist elements that had been so crucial to people like Ranke. Now, confronted by disaster and the ensuing *Weimarzeit* chaos that this seemed to have spawned, Meinecke desperately attempted to preserve the inviolability of the historical individuality by, in essence, redefining what it was. It became, as he saw it, some sort of "spiritual breakthrough . . . in the network of mechanical and biological causalities" (i.e., a cultural singularity), which (unlike the state) embodied universality in an almost pristine form. The historical individuality had become a "moment" of human experience grasped empathetically by the historian in his/her search for universal values. This struck me as absurd. How could one re-experience and then relate "moments," like those in the choral movements of Beethoven's Ninth Symphony or ones to be found in some sort of arcane philosophical "discovery" such as nominalism, things which have no relevance at all to history—most particularly since their appearances represented "breakthroughs"—to the ebb and flow which had to constitute historical movement? Meinecke's efforts to "save" Historicism seemed (and still seem) to be a means of elevating both history and the historian from the slough of political involvement, coincidentally of course, just before World War II.

Yet, as the seminar continued to focus upon Eliade's distinction between "sacred" and "profane" time, a very crucial notion began to emerge, one which struck me with emotional as well as intellectual force. Granted that one cannot somehow bifurcate the *historical process* between material and spiritual elements and then extricate the spiritual as being the "stuff" of real history. Could it not be true, though, that the individual historian has to be hypothesizing and judging out of a sort of timeless niche? To be sure, as all modern historiographers have stated, the historian's judgments and hypotheses are greatly influenced, if not determined, by the age in which he/she lives; hence, Croce's declaration that all history is necessarily contemporary. Nonetheless, in the very act of making some sort of statement about the past, the historian is acting *as if* he/she is standing outside of history. Again, this cannot in fact be happening. Yet a judgment or hypothesis about the past, however provisional it might be (and even if the historian is later compelled to modify or revoke it altogether), would seem to presuppose a willingness to suspend a sense of temporality (i.e., of being "merely" part of a process). The notion that the object of reflection, the past itself, can somehow be divided up between crude patterns of causality and universal cultural breakthroughs is of course, absurd. But, is not every statement about this past a testimony to the historian's faith that this represents such a breakthrough? Is it perhaps *necessary* to see the historian as operating out of, and continuously touching base with, a "sacred space?"

As time went on, I realized that, in referring to "the historian," I was, of course, referring to myself. This was unusual, certainly with regards to my position as a student of history. I have been forced to conclude that in many areas of my life, I certainly have been and am "self-centered." The role of *my-self* in historical judgment however is something that I had never before considered. To be sure, I always realized that those elements of the past that I had chosen to investigate were filtered through the mediating screen of my own experiences. The "screen" itself, however (at least when related to academic life), was something of an abstraction. Matters of experience were crucial in how one related to other people as both they and oneself existed in a contemporaneity to which historical concerns had to be correlated. The sublimated self that was scholar, though, had been set aside, sort of cast out into a world as opaque as possible to "subjective" intrusions. The "screen" would always be there, somehow, but as an unwanted "other," at least with regard to historical scholarship. One accepted it *faut de mieux*, even recognized that it could hardly be extrinsic to historical investigation, yet viewed it as being a subjective impediment to this process.

Throughout the late summer and early fall of 1982, by fits and starts, I became aware that that which allowed me to undertake incursions into the past was a melange of images, fantasies, attractions, and fears that constituted a sort of inviolable core, absolutely immune to rational dissection. These images, fantasies, and so forth were themselves time-bound (*"zeitgebunden,"* as the historicists would put it) in nature. Technology and transport took their points of departure and return from steam locomotives grounded in the realities of youth. A frozen pastiche of gray, wash-line strung tenements and jagged Kirchneresque street scenes served the same function for urban life. Revolutions began and ended with peak-capped Red Guardsmen, clumsily bundled against the November chill, levelling spike-bayonetted rifles at unseen targets. War, in its most ultimately hideous and fascinating qualities, was captured in a camera-like sweep over heavily burdened man-bundles wearily leaving trenches—advancing, falling. It did not matter which armies were thus imagined; the shell-maimed, sullen landscape over which they advanced was, somehow, in an undefined Eastern European locale.

I had been aware of these images for a long time. In fact, several of them had served as convenient reference points during periods of psychotherapy. What my mental journey ("sacred versus profane" time to Historicism to "sacred space") produced was the awareness that, depending on the historical excursion to be undertaken, one or the other of these images (or, of course, others not mentioned) served as referents, even at times partially accompanying me as I went on my way. A particular object of concern and/or analysis might have little (if anything) to do with the time-bound image or fantasy to which in some obscure way it was correlated. Indeed, it might well be representative of a force or development that overthrew the social, technological, or political arrangements of which the image was an expression. Yet, the integrity of the image or fantasy, attraction or fear that sent me back into alien landscapes remained—indeed, had to remain. I have come to learn the source (in a psychogenetic sense) of some of them; the sources of others will remain obscured to me; it does not in the end matter very much. What did matter for me, perhaps most particularly as a historian striving for objectivity, was the existence of a space/time amalgam that I had hallowed, rendered "sacred," and thus shielded against what Eliade called "the terror of history." What statements and judgments about the past I might make, indeed, even the particular aspect(s) of it that I was choosing to investigate might, as mentioned earlier, have nothing to do with my sacred space. Indeed, at times it was imperative that they have nothing at all to do with it. The existence of a timeless (at least in the chronological sense) realm in the end unsullied by any sort of reality that lay outside it, while not exactly the "source" of whatever creative abilities I might have, was of central importance in their articulation.

The Eliade readings thus had brought to the surface something whose relevance I had seen demonstrated only in self-consciously subjective settings—the crucial significance of the distinction between what Freud referred to as "kairotic" and chronological time as a vital, indeed, necessary component of my intellectual life. I was beginning to reconsider the visit to Eastern Europe in light of this "discovery," when Professor Eliade himself arrived at the university in late October, 1982.

I had seen early photographs of him and somehow expected that he would be a burly, bushy-browed sort of individual who smoked a pipe. I was correct only on the last count. I was, however, totally correct in my anticipation that he would be eager to respond to questions and I, along with many others, bombarded him with them. From the general course of the discussions, and most certainly from his public lecture, it became obvious that he, as well as most of those present, was interested in the overarching (to use a deliciously grandiose, Enlightenment variety word) issue of what Western philosophy and science could learn from Eastern spiritual traditions. Yet, and not really out of ignorance of the Eastern traditions, or even lack of interest in them, I found myself focusing in on Western concerns, e.g., millenarianism, with particular emphasis upon the chiliasm of Joachim of Fiore, religion and art in twentieth-century Europe, Western psychology and mysticism, and so forth.

It soon became obvious that, although I stayed away from interwar Romanian issues per se, it was of utmost importance for me to see him in a European, particularly Eastern European, context. Throughout his visit, certain passages from his autobiography kept flashing through my mind. Above all, these concerned what Professor Eliade saw as the singular (almost tragically so) position of Romania between East and West and, related to that, the overpowering feeling that a spiritual "mission" of sorts engendered by this position would never be fulfilled. As has been the case of all peoples with missions of one sort or another, time was of the essence. And, in Romania's case, mundane geopolitical circumstances had made certain that time would be the enemy. It was generally in this context that some very early memories of Professor Eliade came to mind. These concerned Romania's involvement in World War I.

Romania, in pursuance of a foreign policy both avaricious and disastrous, entered the war on the side of the Allies in the summer of 1916. The early successes of General Brusiloff's offensive led her to do so. However, Brusiloff's advance had been contained enough that by the time the Romanian army began to take offensive operations of its own, the Austro-Hungarian, German, and Bulgarian armies had time to focus their attentions upon the Romanian army. What resulted was a military disaster of the first order. The badly equipped and worse led Romanian army was smashed, and Bucharest, indeed most of the country, was occupied. Eliade was but nine years old when Romania entered the war. He was, however, aware of the disasters that had attended this. His response to them was to create an internal war, one in which the Romanian army was consistently victorious. Occasionally, he would hear of "real" victories. However, despite the fact that remnants of the army, after the initial rout, were fighting holding actions of incredible bravery on the Siret River, "victories" were few and far between. Only the general course of the war, which was eventually determined in the West, allowed for the political victory won by Romania after the conflict ended. Yet, in a very real "internal" war, Romania had always won.

It was unclear to me whether the very young, albeit unusually gifted, Eliade was concerned with any sort of Romanian spiritual mission at that time. It seemed to me, though, that he had created for himself a "sacred" space/time dimension in which at least physical victory was assured. There can be little doubt that the fact that his father was an officer in the Romanian army had a great deal to do with this. Perhaps in a more attenuated manner, this also had much to do with Professor Eliade's later, broader view of the Romanian mission. In the end, it did not matter. Whatever its source or sources might have been, there emerged in my reading of Eliade's autobiography the sense of a sacred place, a dimension of cognition and experience that accompanied him wherever he went. Indeed, however dialectically, it was perhaps *responsible* for the journeys undertaken. As I thought of and felt these things, I had to be aware that it was of particular importance for *me* that such a "sacred" *Romanian* space/time exist. I knew that, in many ways, Professor Eliade's spiritual quests had gone far beyond this, and even though I sensed its presence from time to time, I was afraid to ask him about it except in the most indirect ways imaginable. Some comments he made about Chagall's artwork offered an opportunity, but I blew it.

In any case, during the aforementioned public lecture, I was able to put all of my own musings about Eliade the Romanian aside and (despite the poor acoustics and the almost surrealistic presence of a huge photograph of Glenn Miller, who with trombone in hand, gazed down benignly over the scene) learn a great deal. Alas, I also gave vent to some prejudices. At times, I have been interested in the Eastern religions and several of the topics considered by Professor Eliade during his lecture, in particular, the congruence of various cosmologies with some of the more speculative concerns of modern physics were downright enthralling.

It was hardly surprising that large numbers of local Buddhists, Hindus, and others who adhered to less well-defined variants of "Eastern mysticism" were drawn to Eliade's lecture. For a variety of reasons (some of them probably quite irrational), I have always been very suspicious of these folk, and this was articulated in various ill-tempered asides (usually for the benefit of Anne Marie, who was not particularly impressed). "Look at that pious fraud over there!" I'd say, apropos of nothing. "He got a C— in German history! He's helpless without his prayer wheel!" Or, "Jesus Christ! Look at those gaping buffoons over there on the left! I'll bet those goddamned ignoramuses don't know what the hell he's talking about!" (A bad reaction to have to own up to, I suppose, but, it was there.) Generally, I thought (and still think) that what Professor Eliade had to say was very clear to me, although obviously, the readings and the marvelous seminar gave me quite an advantage over probably quite a few in the audience.

I filled a note-pad with scribblings. Yet, afterwards I had to confess that, if indeed at least some of those of whom I'd probably been unjustifiedly contemptuous were off into irrelevancies, I had in part been in a world of my own as well. For, from time to time, I found myself correlating not so much what he said, but the figure (or *presence*) of Professor Eliade himself to various utterly irrelevant issues. I would focus on him, close my eyes and see, frozen in the mist of late afternoon, a Polish farmer in peaked cap sitting in a horse-drawn cart piled with potatoes, staring up at our train as it swept past him. A discussion of recent speculations in astro-geophysics would cause me to try, somehow, to focus upon the speaker's eyes, and then I would "see" the dark, mustachioed Romanian peasant with fur hat, colorful vest, wide belt and boots standing in the train aisle, sharing cigarettes with a soldier, dressed in that tightly fitting green uniform that brought to mind the army of Stalin's Russia. At one point, a particular intonation in Professor Eliade's voice faded into the atonal chanting of two male country people who, seated in a cafe in Bucharest and very drunk, were *singing* stories of the day's events to each other, sort of like "tale-bearers" of years past. My wife and I had been enchanted; the waiter had not. Then for some reason or another, my mind's eye was traversed by a softly panting Bulgarian steam locomotive in green trim and running gear—someone had painted a picture of Donald Duck on the tender. The lecture ended, and we joined the crowd in applause. It had been an unusual experience.

Of course, once Professor Eliade's visit was over, it did not take terribly long to sort out what the strictly personal impact of *it* (the readings and the seminar) had been. For better or worse, I had been brought face-to-face with something whose psychogenetic existence I had always been aware of, but whose reality as the very core of *all* my intellectual involvements I had either overlooked or chosen not to see. Without my own immutable realm, my "sacred space," infused with that "time" generic to it (something whose *form*, if not content, I generously chose to assign to historians in general), there could not be any explorations of the past. Without an ahistorical domain, something that in its total immunity to change was ultimately real to me, there could be no dealing with change at all, no historical reality. In a word, what the "Eliade experience" (in all of its various forms) had made me see, was the *concreteness* of what one would have to call an aspect of religiosity (if not strictly speaking "religion") and the efficacy of such in "profane" intellectual pursuits. Furthermore, as indicated earlier, it occurred to me that, in some way, these pursuits were paradoxical *articulations* of that which was (to me) "sacred," although, except in the most attenuated psychoanalytical sense, the precise relationship remained obscure.

When Professor Eliade himself arrived, I was confronted with the individual whose work had been so extraordinarily meaningful with regards to this dimension of self-discovery. Of course, even in my most wildly solipsistic moments, I had to realize that others might very well have made similar discoveries, and perhaps more on their own; but I was, for the moment, concerned only with my own project. Because Professor Eliade himself came from the part of the world that, for one or the other reason, was so crucial to the "sacred" inner core of my own emotional and cognitive life, it became important for me to see him in a certain context, or perhaps more accurately, to see a certain context *in him*. Trying to discover a determinate Eastern European sacred space/time within him had been the self-centered means by which I had sought to further illuminate my own more reified fantasy-bound space/time. I had been trying to "go home again," borne by steam engines of childhood memory, but into a house that had never been mine.

Now, separated from the "Eliade experience" by almost a year and a half, I cannot point to any obvious changes that it has made in my approaches to life and to my work. Yet, I know that changes have occurred. I am, in this regard, reminded of a description of the first atomic reaction, which I read when about 11 years old or so in a book concerned with introducing children to the magical world of atomic energy. Under the circumstances, it seems only appropriate that, as we know, this first atomic reaction took place in November 1942 under the bleachers of Stagg Field, at the University of Chicago. The description went something like this: The fuel was put into the reactor. There was no sign of anything taking place. There was no fire. When the fuel was taken out, it looked just as it had when it had been put in. But something very important had happened.

EDWARD P. NOLAN

The Forbidden Forest: Eliade as Artist and Shaman

In that diaspora known as the academic world, Mircea Eliade is one of our necessary angels: angel, here, in the more sombre, Rilkean, even Islamic, sense as well as in the more pedestrian sense of Broadway backer. Perhaps that is why the range of attitude among academics regarding Eliade and his contribution is so wildly divergent: It ranges from a deep respect for his groundbreaking scholarly works and a collegial (if at times grudging) admiration for his stupendous success as a socratic teacher-provocateur to bona-fide, far-ranging query and criticism concerning the nature and methodology of his discipline, the history of religions, which he created nearly single-handedly at the University of Chicago over the past three decades. There is a less lovely spectrum of reception that ranges from noncritical hero-worship to mean-spirited, even vicious *ad hominem* attacks most of us would rather read in wicked academic novels than in academic journals. Some of this ambivalence among scholars is due to a concerted inattention to an important body of his work that, once assessed, helps us triangulate more satisfactorily his contribution to our time—I refer to his considerable literary production.

This short essay will attempt a prolegomenon, a map to explore the illuminating relationships that obtain between fictive constructs reflecting inner vision, and academic texts claiming verifiable fidelity to the inherited structures of common day. During his spectacular career, Eliade offered us an intriguing set of challenges. Part of the arsenal required for meeting those challenges can be found sequestered in the silence of implication generated by the many differing voices in and through which he has spoken over the years.

Looking back, World War II seems to have generated almost as many books as babies, yet only a small number of those books helped shape the thinking of the next generation. Surely one of them was Eliade's *Myth of the Eternal Return,* or, as titled in the paperback edition, *Cosmos and History.* Eliade both fascinated us with his visions of the cosmos, and disturbed us with his meditations on history. Although the generation of the fifties had gained a reasonably just reputation for apathy, many were deeply shocked by the last essay in the book, "The Terror of History" (reprinted earlier on in this volume).

In a world recently and at great cost made free for democracy, this essay brought bad news. It insisted that man had one last choice: Christ or nihilism. Although many of us felt we had found a heroic book, we were at the same time abashed at liking everything about it but its ending, and liking even less the way in which that ending seemed to proceed with such fatal, logical necessity out of all that went before. There was, in addition, a grim and unrelenting tone in the closing pages that seemed at first to clash discordantly with the optimistic and generous vision pervading the rest of the book. Let me try to recapture that sense of things by means of a brief quotation. I choose a passage in which Eliade seems to deny the possibility of any real marriage between a modern scientific view of history and authentic, existential freedom:

> Modern man's boasted freedom to make history is illusory for nearly the whole of the human race. At most, man is left free to choose between two positions: (1) to oppose the history that is being made by the very small minority (and, in this case, he is free to choose between suicide and deportation); (2) to take refuge in a subhuman existence or in flight.[1]

There is a particular voice speaking here and we attend with some care. It is the voice of one of the most gifted men in his country, speaking in Paris in 1949. It is a voice speaking for, but no longer in, Romania for which the atomic bomb could not be justified by its ends, for it had ended nothing. Romania, with the tacit assistance of the Allies, simply passed from one untenable dictatorship to another. As we in the mid-eighties read and re-read these sentences, we must engage in the always necessary journey through the labyrinths of time and listen to a man in his early forties, *nel' mezzo del cammin di nostra vita,* in love with the West that had betrayed his people, and dogged by all the interior as well as exterior indignities and humilities of exile (recall Dante again: "how salt the bread, how steep the up and down of someone else's stairs"). We assess and, if we can, assent to the authenticity of that voice. We do that even as we see from our later temporal vantage the operation of one of Eliade's great ironic themes. He says, and

embodies it by saying it then and there, "History matters, not because
it means anything, but because it maims and kills. To fail to resist the
crushing pressures of such meaningless history is to fail to live a
significant life." The cosmic irony, as usual, grins like the Cheshire cat,
for all attempts to offer meaningful resistance to the monster of history
are only possible in the hot web and onrush of the very history one
is attempting to negate.

A toleration of this mixture of anger and love, of contempt and hope,
is requisite to reaching an acceptable reading of his summary argument,
which is couched in a civility for which he has in time become an
emblem:

> It must not be forgotten that, if Abraham's faith can be defined as "for God
> everything is possible," the faith of Christianity implies that everything is
> also possible for man. . . . Faith, in this context . . . means absolute
> emancipation from any kind of natural 'law' and hence the highest freedom
> that man can imagine. . . . Only such a freedom . . . is able to defend
> modern man from the terror of history—a freedom, that is, which has its
> source and finds its guaranty and support in God.[2]

What is the nature and direction of the pilgrimage that is here implied?
Does Eliade so despise the contingencies of history and so hotly desire
freedom that to exorcise the one and retrieve the other he demands a
sellout to God? Surely not. This is not a fundamentalist Tertullian
trumpet blast signalling the cessation of further discourse but an un-
flinching challenge to his listeners to respond.

We are left at the end of *Cosmos and History* not with an answer,
but a question, and the question is this: can we deal with Eliade? What
is the inventory of modes through which we can counter the alienating
effects of history as it destroys our sense of meaning by ever increasing
the barrier of distance between ourselves and our founding and com-
memorating origins? Are there ways to live responsibly in history without
standing for Christ? Or engaging in hallucinogens? Or succumbing to
archaic sensibility? Is there a scenario for a cure of the terror that
engages rather than abandons the faculties of memory and reason? The
questions raised in the silence following the closure of *Cosmos and
History* begin to be answered in the other voices through and in which
Eliade speaks to us, not only across decades, but as recently as yesterday.

Governing moments of the mind are periodic and run their course.
Eliade's intellectual honesty spoke unequivocally then and was one with
the end of his book—but surely not one with the end of his thinking.
After *Cosmos and History* he worked on his extraordinary book on
shamanism. That in turn was interrupted by an irresistible need to write

fiction. Thus 1949 also saw the beginning of the five years needed to complete his epic novel *The Forbidden Forest*. The answers we seek lie somewhere in the dialectic between scientific research and literary creativity, between the analytic and synthetic moments of the mind, between the diurnal and nocturnal worlds of the intellect and the imagination.

Thus I propose to examine the confrontation with art as a possible scenario for curing history's terror and I shall use Eliade's most important novel as my primary exemplum. I will consider the confrontation with art with the help of Eliade's analytics, as a second-level initiation rite in which both the writer and the reader, in mutual imaginative sympathy, engage in a scenario of catastrophe and restoration. Finally, to show how centered this view of things really is, I shall indicate the affiliation this kind of thinking has with a tradition that goes back beyond Ovid and Virgil to Aristotle. Let me begin with a sense of how *The Forbidden Forest* reads and then move on to a sense of how it works.

It is a large canvas, centering in Bucharest just before, during, and just after World War II. It also ranges out into the Romanian countryside and as far as a light-drenched Lisbon, a Paris consisting of several rooms, a door and a desk, and a London blacked-out under air attack. Starting on one night of St. John's and ending on another, it moves majestically, with alternating moments of high comedy, psychological paralysis, soaring lyricism, bureaucratic pettifoggery, and terrifying brutality. Like certain novels of Henry James, which also have such epic sweep and reach, this novel is populated by scarcely more than a dozen people. This results in an ultimately functional sense of both arbitrariness and necessity, of richness and economy, and a pervasive echo of a voice crying in the wilderness.

The central character, Stefan, seems quite capable of handling the more meaningless chores of getting through the day or the job, but his hold on things diminishes as the stakes are raised. We are drawn to him, but find him difficult to understand. The narrator is not always helpful, though the voice seems reliable enough. Stefan is engaged in a number of activities that we learn about from other characters but on which the narrator remains silent. Our grasp of the facts of Stefan's world is less than absolute. Yet Stefan's story is the major running thread of the narrative. He seems to have had a premonition involving a lady and a car. He is not clear about the vision though he speaks of it often. The narrator reports Stefan's conversations about the vision but is of no additional assistance in explaining it.

Stefan bears a striking resemblance to a contemporary Romanian writer in the novel and each man is at times mistaken for the other—the writer, in fact, is assassinated by just such a mistake. Although Stefan

is in love with two women (and married to one of them), the result
is incapability, for one surface reason or another, of being happy with
either of them. His quest seems to involve both a search for and
avoidance of these women. A parallel concern of Stefan's is a near
obsession with history as a trap of meaninglessness, and he engages
in intermittent searches for ways of escaping the deadening effects of
the quotidian. His wife dies in an air attack. His feverish search for
Ileana, the other woman, succeeds in a forest outside Paris. He and
Ileana decide they must part. In the course of driving to a train station
so that Stefan can depart forever, they are instead forever joined in a
car crash. The car is, of course, the same car present in Stefan's mind
in his clairvoyant vision twelve years earlier at the beginning of the
novel.

There are several compellingly depicted characters who form a con-
stellation of relationships that surrounds and gives a sense of shape to
the enigmatic hero at the center. One of these characters is a consumptive
philosopher named Biris. Biris reports Stefan's preoccupation with history:

History has taken revenge on him. He has a phobia against history. He has
a horror of events. He'd like things to stand still the way they seemed to
do in the paradise of his childhood. So history takes its revenge and buries
him as often as it can. It throws him into the detention camp by mistake.
It kills men in his place, always by mistake. And so on.[3]

Stefan, in a bombing raid in London, echos the closing pages of *Cosmos and History*:

> History is invigorating and fertile only for those who make it, not for those who endure it. Take the British aviator who defends the English sky and risks his life at every moment. For him, naturally, contemporary history is productive, because the history he makes aids him in self-revelation. But for us, for all the others who watch passively from the ground, his struggle against the German aviators—what does this struggle reveal to us? Only terror. (p. 250)

Finally, as Biris much later lies dying under the torture of post-war communist intelligence agents (who also worked for the Gestapo during the war) he suggests what he would have liked to say to the existentialists at the *Deux Magots* had he made it out to Paris:

> I'd want to bring them a kind of message of love and farewell. . . . So they'll know that even though they've condemned us to death, we fools and paupers here still love and venerate them. Because the West is there—where the sun sets. That's where the true twilight is and it's more beautiful there than here. Only there, in the West, do people realize that they die. That's why in the West men love History—because it reminds them continually that men are mortal and civilizations are mortal. We who live here don't have much reason to love History. Why should we love it? For ten centuries History meant for us the barbarian invasions. For another five centuries it meant the Turkish terror. And now for I don't know how many centuries History will imply Soviet Russia. . . . (p. 529)

History is a remorseless trap and becomes a theme that competes for our attention with the hero who seeks to avoid it but can only find his fulfillment in it.

There are a number of disparate details that haunt the novel—their repetition in flashbacks and moments of recollection render them portentous: a pair of gloves; a dead tooth; a putative Rubens; a library of common wisdom; a wood-eating insect called, ominously enough, the Death-Clock; and a brother and sister who drowned long ago, quite near the shore, entangled in weeds. The putative Rubens causes, albeit indirectly, death and other disasters, but is then lost or stolen and never heard of again. The pair of gloves surfaces again and again through the novel and never appears to belong to anyone. The insect quietly eats the furniture, and the brother and sister, after being recollected several times, rest, after all, in peace. The repeated detail that promises significance but reneges on that promise acts as a literary image for those bits of history that so easily cause crippling obsession. There are special spaces that promise revelations: a cellar in provincial Zinca, Prof. Antim's salon, the Cathedral at Ulm, and *Sambo*, a memorable locked room of Stefan's childhood (the *Sambo* selection is reprinted elsewhere in this volume). The revelations never come. Some details seem special, others very ordinary—it becomes impossible to tell the difference.

Finally, there are a number of moments in which the narrative is interrupted for the purpose of depicting a complex image that, by repeated later reference, begins to have a semi-autonomous life and function of its own.

> He brought wildflowers for Catalina that he had gathered from the edges of the vacant lots and from the fallow fields behind the cemetery. They were small and dusty with faded colors, almost dry. Once as he was entering the cemetery with a larger nosegay—on his way he had met a gypsy selling flowers—he suddenly remembered the painting in Stefan's study: the black glove and the long stemmed wildflowers thrown down in haste on a little table. "She had just returned from a long walk . . . when she heard the telephone ringing," Stefan's words came back to him, "She has run to answer it. . . . I'm still waiting for her. . . ." (p. 427)

There is the strategic resonance with Joyce and especially Proust: the character sees one image before him which in turn calls up, in stereoscopic juxtaposition, a like, yet tellingly different, image from the past. The image from the past is a moment captured in art, a slice of existential, recollected time frozen into the artificial, but more lasting "slow time" of Keats' grecian urn. The two images, one from the past and the realm of art, the other from the realm of the narrative present, occasion metaphoric meditation; the juxtaposition insists, for a moment, on some hidden identity. These resonances are important because they link Eliade to his proper contexts of Western tradition. More important, however, is the way in which the passage "freezes" all the various implied temporal moments into one image: the narrated now, a prior narrated then, an even earlier moment of the picture's interpretation by Stefan, the implied moments of the picture's purchase, its painting, and, by imagining the lady that isn't there, a moment of the painter's life that was transformed by the artist into the painting in the first place. The quoted passage is thus an image of the forwarding principles of the novel in which we find it. The function of such self-reflexive images is to help us better read and understand both the text and the world the text implies.

The Latin *textus* means a weaving or a web. Everything indicates *The Forbidden Forest* constitutes just such a text. The double-plot of search and avoidance; the alternating atmospherics; the lack of total reliability regarding the narrator; the obsession with history as a trap; the nagging, repeated, yet insignificant detail; the promising rooms and spaces that open up to reveal nothing; and the *regressus ad absurdam* images of self-reflexion all teach us to read *The Forbidden Forest* as a labyrinthine web of time as well as space. Not for nothing is "labyrinth" one of the repeated catch-words used as a kind of fraternal password between Stefan and Biris: "I have returned from the labyrinth"; "I have brought word from the labyrinth." It is probably true that the term 'labyrinth' is currently over-fashionable, but one must remember that the figure of the labyrinth is not important because it is fashionable, but fashionable because it is important. It is at least as old as the ship at sea, the body in the house, or the descent into hell as a basic informing metaphor of the situation in which we find ourselves. Why is it such a powerful figure, what needs does it answer?

The complete labyrinth requires not only a complex structure with an easy entry and difficult exit but also a minotaur at the center and a Theseus who wants to find it, kill it, and escape. Each element requires the others for its own fulfillment. From the point of view of process, Theseus only becomes intelligible to himself (as well as to others, those observers for whom he acts as surrogate) as he seeks the center and its devouring beast. As he moves, he maps the plot of the labyrinth in which he moves. From the point of view of structure, the labyrinth, in this case the plot of the novel, by offering impedance, or resistance, allows the energy-impelling character to fulfill itself by revealing its shape, much as the glow of the wire reveals and fulfills, in heat and light, the electricity passing through it. Like the door in Kafka's "Parable of the Law" in *The Trial*, the labyrinth has only one function: to reveal, by completing his presence, the existential authenticity of the Theseus who seeks to undo it. It is the very inextricability of interdependency between Theseus and his labyrinth, between hero and plot, between text and context, between ourselves and our world, that constitutes the subject of discovery during the confrontation at the center.

He saw the parapet, and beyond it he could picture the abyss that yawned in the darkness. He began to tremble. I have to tell her. I still have time to tell her! But the headlights of a car lifted them out of the darkness, blinding him, and instinctively he drew closer to Ileana. That moment—unique, infinite—revealed to him the total beatitude he had yearned for so many years. It was there in the glance she bestowed on him, bathed in tears. He had known from the beginning this was the way it would be. He had known that, feeling him very near her, she would turn her head and look at him. He had known that this last moment, this moment without end, would suffice. (p. 596)

The minotaur, whatever else it is, will, if perceived carefully enough by Theseus, reveal itself as a fulfilling mirror, as the completion of the self in the other. This final awareness of the supreme authentication of the self in the absolute and undeniable presence of the other is what the Middle Ages styled the fruit of love, and is what Stefan and Ileana see in one another's eyes as they drive over the cliff. This is the shock of beatific recognition that vindicates the initiatory ordeals suffered by the characters within the novel. And the depiction of that moment acts as a fulfilling and revelatory mirror to the reader outside, whose very act of imaginatively (and temporarily) appropriating Eliade's massive novel as the real world constitutes an ordeal of initiation of his own. It is important to see that Eliade does not tell us any of this, nor does he merely show or demonstrate it. He constructs a novel that demands a certain kind of active reading, the successful performance of which brings the reader forward, in the full use of intellect and memory, toward greater understanding. Any increase in the light diminishes the terror.

I hope this miniature impression of *Forbidden Forest* can fill a double function. First, to give some first sense of the experience one has when reading the novel and second, to show the way in which an active, aggressive reading involves an imaginative projection of the writer: if I were writing this, what would I be up to? It is a relation of mutual sympathy. The writer also conjures up some imaginative double of the reader: If I were reading this, what would I be up to? The act of reading is done, I would argue, in an attitude of active, participatory assent that, if brought off at all well, results in an ascent to an alternative world. Such an act of reading is as celebratory as it is analytic. The act of reading is always multiple: one looks *at* as well as *through* the words, one feels as one thinks, one puts the work together even as one takes it apart. The mutuality of engagement on the part of both agents of reality (writer and reader, each being themselves while imagining the other) eventuates in a figure-dance of minds across whatever time or space may intervene. This is surely what Plato has Socrates mean when he argues with Phaedrus that right discourse is tantamount to right loving. This is what Ovid shouts as he closes the Metamorphoses with *vivam*.

Why do we keep reading such complicated and difficult novels? Perhaps to feel better. We may read our novels in the privacy of our bedrooms but that in no way changes the fact that all serious reading is a collective enterprise. As Aristotle argues in the *Poetics*, something civilizing happens in the act of participating in the creation of secondary worlds. Whether the particular secondary world is "true" or not is itself not at issue. Although the text of the *Poetics* is faulty, Aristotle argues that the worst thing that can go wrong with a citizen is to be too easily attracted or too easily repelled: Such citizens are too easily moved, pity and fear are present in excess. He also argues that the collective function of the Athenian state theater was to gather the citizens together so that by imaginative participation, by a process involving interior and sympathetic resonance with the exterior imitative structures of drama, they could exercise the passions of pity and fear. Such disciplined exercise, Aristotle implies, results in a therapeutic catharsis, exorcises the excess presence of these passions by the very exercising of them. It is a matter of establishing appropriate balance of conflicting passions rather than eliminating them altogether. For Aristotle, then, the fundamental justification for the art of the theater is not aesthetic, but homeopathically therapeutic. To participate as an audience in the Dionysian theater was to undergo an ordeal that led to increased health in the face of the world.

To return to Eliade, his recent lecture (reprinted elsewhere in this volume) entitled "Waiting for the Dawn" echos Aristotle's justification of theater as therapy:

> His physical pains and psychomental disorders represent a series of initiatory ordeals: his symbolic death is always followed by a "resurrection" or a "rebirth" manifested by his radical cure and by the appearance of a new, more structured, stronger personality.[4]

Eliade goes on to suggest the conceivability that:

> . . . interest in shamanism and the awareness of the psychomental risks involved in hallucinogens may have another consequence in the near future: helping contemporary Western man undergo sickness . . . as a series of initiatory ordeals.[5]

I would argue, perhaps more strongly than Eliade might wish to hear, that in addition to confrontations with hallucinogens, careful confrontations with art can also function as useful "scenarios of the shaman," can help us work through our cultural "sickness." I have been suggesting all along, in fact, that Eliade, as author of the novel *Forbidden Forest*, has functioned for his readers as an Aristotelian shaman, a master of revels. To work through his novel as a journey through the labyrinth is itself an initiatory ordeal. Attending to Eliade's orchestrations of image, theme, and structure evokes a balanced mixture of irony and sympathy that helps us achieve the required middle distance between ourselves and the world of the novel we imagine for a moment as our own. This generation of a balance between the sense of distance occasioned by irony and the sense of proximity achieved by sympathy is a move toward greater health, toward a "new, more structured, stronger personality," with which we can better face the "terror of history."

If Eliade functions as a second-level shaman, his novel is the "trick" that engages the patient reader. And the mutual desire of shaman and patient, of writer and reader, to imagine their opposite in this interchange comes close to what I suppose was meant in the Middle Ages by the term "charity." Art does not, of course, in itself contain the vision, the revelation, the "heavens, the hells, the longed-for lands," but it can bring us to the brink of revelation and that is going a great distance. We may neither need nor wish for more.

Finally, I would like to "place" Eliade and his novel in a particular perspective vis-à-vis the mainstream of Western literary tradition. It may seem perverse to insist that an intellectual maverick such as Eliade, speaking in exile as a citizen of a small country whose own history has been at the mercy of major conflicting powers, should in any way be considered in the mainstream. And yet the mainstream of our tradition flows uninterrupted from the narrative of exiled Odysseus in search of Ithaca. Eliade, a life-long quester in exile, is both poet and theoretician of the outsider, and can appropriately be seen as linked not only to such modern connoisseurs of chaos and experts in futility as Dostoevsky, Kafka, Proust, Joyce, Mann, and Singer, but also, ironically, to their precursors operating in that namesake of Romania: Augustan Rome. We close, then, with a brief pas-de-trois: I present, for inspection, a few key images from *The Forbidden Forest* and suggest how we can sense in them the echoes of a line of filiation that runs back to Ovid and Virgil. Thus we can see just how deeply anchored in tradition Mircea Eliade, master of an ironic yet positive stoicism, turns out to be.

In the middle of the novel, Stefan has an illuminating vision which we do not witness, but which we hear him report to his counter figure, the consumptive philosopher Biris:

> "You know," Stefan resumed abruptly, "when I was there in the labyrinth I felt closed in on all sides. I was like a captive in a huge metal sphere. I didn't feel anymore that I was in the belly of the whale. I was inside an immense metal sphere. I didn't see the limits anywhere, but I felt I was locked hopelessly in it. I felt that no matter how much I might struggle, no matter how far I might go forward . . . I couldn't reach those iron walls. . . . I felt condemned for the rest of my life to whirl blindly, vainly, inside that sphere which was like a dark labyrinth. And yet one day . . . I broke through the wall and came out as if I had emerged from an enormous egg, an egg with an impregnable shell, invulnerable as stone. But it was a shell that broke at a mere touch and I came out again into the light." (p. 204)

This radical transformation of the image in the eye of the beholder, which triggers both illumination and acceptance, echos many similar moments in the great literature of revelation in change. One such moment occurs near the end of Ovid's *Metamorphoses*, in which Vertumnus, the radiantly handsome god of the changing year, is wooing disinterested Pomona. In order to trick her into love, he comes disguised as an old woman with tales to tell which he hopes will convince the nymph to yield to her lover, who is, of course, none other than himself:

> When the god in the form of age had pleaded in vain, he returned to the form of youth, put off the old woman's rags and stood revealed, as when the sun conquers the clouds and shines clear. He was ready for rape, but needed no force. The nymph, faced with the beauty of the god, answered his passion. (*Meta.*, XIV, 765–771, my translation)

She accepts in love the beauty of the changing year even as it strips itself of disguise and reveals its power. We are left with the haunting nuptial image of the nymph of Rome embracing change as her lover. Stefan's vision of the transformation of the claustrophobia of the metal sphere to the freedom of rebirth out of a cosmic egg constitutes a similar revelation of the miracle of change and its power of release. In these revelations of release and freedom in change we always see concurrent intimations of death as transformation's radical, fulfilling, and hence redemptive figure.

As *The Forbidden Forest* moves toward its striking closure, the political pressures of post-Nazi terrorism in Romania close in on Biris and he is brutally tortured by the interrogators of the state (the regime shifts, the interrogators remain the same: *plus ça change . . . plus c'est la même chose*). As the pain increases to unbearable levels, we have a sense of white-hot iron walls falling in on us and suddenly, unaccountably, beautifully, Biris sings:

> Down from the flowering
> Wild mountain garden
> Threshold of paradise
> Three flocks of sheep
> Come along the path
> Descending to the valley

What seems a lyrical, hallucinogenic loss of control begins to show itself as something richer and more powerful:

> "It's a coded message and it's for Paris. All messages go to Paris. The ships take them. They only travel at night, without lights, but they all go to Paris.

To the West. *Salve Occidens!*" "You're mad!" cried Duma. "You're ridiculing us!" "All messages begin like this—'Down from the flowering wild mountain garden, threshold of paradise . . .' But you can't decipher them if you don't have the key, and you won't find the key except on the ship. When you wake up on the ship, you realize that you're going to Paris. Everyone will be there in the shadow of the lily. . . ." (p. 536)

The end of Biris' ordeal concludes in his death. After the singing, there is the shift from movement to stillness:

" . . . Viorica," murmured Biris. "Tell her I wanted to go to Paris." He smiled and turned to face the monk. Reaching for his hand, he held it tightly in both of his. "Absolve me, Father," he said in a surprisingly clear voice. "Hurry!" . . . "A prayer," Biris whispered. "Say a prayer. . . . Hurry . . ." "You say it too." Bursuc raised his head slowly. "Say it with me . . . 'Our father, which art in Heaven . . .'"

Biris nodded assent, repeating the words slowly and with increasing effort. When the door opened and Doamna Porumbache rushed into the room he tried to raise himself on his elbows. His face brightened suddenly and he smiled. Doamna Porumbache screamed—a startled cry that was stifled as she froze with her hand over her mouth. Irina fell on her knees beside the bed. Happy, at peace, Biris gazed at them with eyes that saw no more. (p. 543)

This scene of music in the face of brutal terror and a shift from pain to frozen quietude evokes a similar image in Ovid that occurs near the end of the narrative of Orpheus. On returning to the realm of the living without Euridice, Orpheus decides to sing only songs of inverted love. As he continues to do so, he arouses the wrath of the maenads who fall upon him (as they fell upon Pentheus) and tear him apart:

. . . the limbs lay scattered about, but the head and the lyre, wonderfully, floated mid-stream, the lyre sounding mournful notes, the lifeless tongue mournful song, mournfully the banks replied . . . and gained the shore of Lesbos. . . . Here the head lay naked upon a foreign shore, a terrible serpent attacked it, locks still dripping from the ocean's spray. But Phoebus came, drove off the snake, right in the act of biting, and froze to stone, just as they were, the open, stretched-out jaws. (*Meta.* XI, 50–60)

As shown above, Eliade's secondary hero, Biris, like Orpheus, incurs the wrath of the maenads, represented in the novel by the interrogators of the regime. As they tear him apart, he suffers a sea change like that of Orpheus and continues, miraculously, to sing in the face of his torturers, until, by the freezing of his eyes, we sense release, death, and a new freedom.

What Eliade and Ovid teach us by these petrefactions of the image is that the problem is not with the dragon, the threatened singing head, nor with the frozen gaze of Biris, but in that our first relationships with such images is one of spurious identity. We first see the image as the thing. The transformations to stone and ice occasion a discovery that increases both our sense of control and our sense of distance: We see that the thing we see is not the thing itself, but an image of the thing. This is the self-correcting process of literature. Its very act of imaging forth helps us to see ourselves in a more appropriate context. The discovery that attends the metamorphoses of the image from kinesis into stasis, from life into death, allows us some release from suffering while simultaneously validating it by transforming a fleeting moment of meaningless personal agony into a more lasting image of impersonal, yet significant form.

If Ovid is the bard of transformation, Virgil is the poet of absence. I spoke of an ironic, but positive stoicism in Eliade. He joins the Ovidian exultations in the restorative powers of radical change, with the darker awareness occasioned by more Virgilian images of absence and hopeless desire. Recall again the image of the painting that haunts Stefan's imagination, a still-life of a bouquet of wildflowers on a table, with a lady's glove lying next to them. He imagines the owner of the glove has been called to the phone, and says, "She's run to answer it . . . I'm still waiting for her." The glove and the wildflowers act so powerfully because they accomplish two important things simultaneously: They establish the existence of the desired lady even as they declare her eternal absence. Eliade's repetition of this image as a kind of leitmotif then musically reinforces our elegiac sense of absence and unanswered desire.

In Book Six of Virgil's *Aeneid*, when Aeneas is about to cross over into hell proper, he sees all the souls of the dead that have not yet received burial and hence are kept from crossing the bar. Here is the line containing the image: *tendebanque manus ripae ulterioris amore* (their hands stretched out in love for the farther shore). This gesture of reaching out in desire, but not in hope, is a master image that embodies the entire ethical gestalt of the *Aeneid*. That Dante read this line with care is clear when he has his own Virgil explain his presence in limbo by saying: We are here, not because we have sinned, but because we did not know: *Vivemmo senza spema in desio* (we live without hope in desire). In *Forbidden Forest*, the painting of the glove and the wildflowers, which Stephan reads as a reminder of both the existence and the absence of the desired woman, is an analogue of Virgil's image of the unburied dead: the eyes of our mind are forever reaching out for the desired lady, even as the arms of the dead reach out for the farther shore: without hope, yet in desire.

All of these images in Ovid, Virgil, and Eliade embody a stoic awareness that accepts the futility of human action in an entropic universe even as it yields to the compelling necessity to engage in human action in spite of that knowledge. It is, I suspect, precisely that ironic balance of knowledge and ignorance that must be present before any action can claim authenticity, whether in pre-Christian Rome, or in post-Christian Bucharest, Paris, Chicago, or Boulder, Colorado.

The golden bough was of vivid metal, its leaves clattered in the wind (*sic leni crepitabat brattea vento*). It partook of the orders of nature and artifice, of life and death. By appropriating the golden bough, Aeneas could descend to his illuminations in hell. I would suggest that the golden bough is an internal mirror-figure of the *Aeneid* as a whole, and as Aeneas took up the bough, we take up the *Aeneid*, the *Metamorphoses*, or *Ulysses*, *The Trial*, or *The Forbidden Forest* as a token of initiation, as the key of entry to the portals of our own journeys through the labyrinth, in that necessary, ceaseless search for the beast at the center: ourselves.

Notes

1. M. Eliade, *Myth of the Eternal Return* (Princeton, NJ: Princeton University Press, 1954), Bollingen Series, pp. 156–157.

2. Ibid., pp. 160–161.

3. M. Eliade, *The Forbidden Forest* (Notre Dame, IN: Notre Dame Press, 1981), p. 214. Further page references will be integrated into the text.

4. Excerpted from Eliade lecture, "Waiting for the Dawn," given at the University of Colorado, Boulder, October 26, 1982.

5. Ibid.

RODNEY L. TAYLOR

——————§§——————

Mircea Eliade: The Self and the Journey

I

The self seems to most of us to be something that is often known primarily for the apparent concreteness of its quality of being. It is a thing, it has definable characteristics, it has the nature of being. Yet it is also something in process, undergoing in each moment countless changes and transformations that create of its perimeters the sense of a journey. Change and transformation become then of the essence in the task of discovering the meaning of the self, a self never quite capable of isolation in the static moment, but glimpsed as through a glass darkly in perpetual peregrination.

Human consciousness has reflected upon the enigma of the self in many times and in many ways. Frequently the metaphor brought to mind is that of the river—it represents continuity and constancy, yet it also represents change and transformation. For some it is a paradox, for others it is the very essence of the adumbration of the self. Locked in mystery and yet partially revealed, there is continuity to the self, yet there is constant change of the self. The Buddhist monk Nagasena tried to explain to the Greek king Menander something of the paradox of the self caught in the process of change. The question was posed as to whether the mature individual is the same as the infant he once was. The monk's answer shows the subtlety of the identification of the self. On the one hand, the mature individual is judged a different self from the self of the infant, as follows by common sense. On the other hand, if the self of the mature individual is truly different from that of the infant, then that mature individual can be said to have had no parents to nourish him and no teachers to instruct him. Thus in one respect he is no longer the infant he once was, or for that matter, he is no longer the self he was in the moment before the present moment. The answer given by Nagasena simply suggests that to recognize the individual one must conclude he is neither the same nor different than he was at previous moments of his life.

For some there is self-consciousness of the movement and process of life, and for a few there is an effort made to penetrate the process of movement of the life to discover what meaning might be attributed to the life itself. The attempt to penetrate the process and thereby punctuate particular moments for their meaning and significance for the totality of the processes of the life is what, when written, can properly be called autobiography. Others have eloquently expressed the nature of the autobiographical task. Pascal, for example, has said that autobiography "involves the reconstruction of the movement of a life, or part of a life, in the actual circumstances in which it was lived. Its center of interest is the self, not the outside world, though necessarily the outside world must appear so that, in give and take with it, the personality finds its peculiar shape."[1] It is the attempt to understand given moments, and, within the context of the movement from moment to moment, to measure the cumulative process of the life.

The process of punctuating particular moments and adjudicating them within the framework of the process of the life must also ultimately depend upon the particular perspective of the individual as he engages in the task of self-articulation. In other words, autobiography is not only deriving meaning from the experience of particular moments of the past, but it is also viewing those moments from the point at which one engages in the task of writing the autobiography itself. Thus we might well say that there is a standpoint from which the life is viewed. The standpoint is the perspective of the self at the moment at which the autobiographical journey is begun. This perspective provides to a degree a framework for the interpretation and understanding of the moving moments of the life process. There is, after all, potentially an infinite complexity to the diverse moments of a life and yet we see in the autobiographical task a process of selection that yields ultimately the meaning in the movement of the life itself. It is well to remember that not all moments of the life are brought to mind in the autobiography. Only certain moments become the focus of attention. Were every moment to be recalled in full detail we would have a story as long as the life itself. Obviously that does not happen. Were there to be a kind of outline of all activities and all events, while we might have a manageable amount of material, we would not have autobiography so much as simply a chronicle of events. Selection then is of salient import to the construction of autobiography.

What determines the selection of particular points over others? Why are certain events recalled and others not? Often when one compares

biography and autobiography it appears as if the individual described
is two entirely different people. Why? It is simply the case that what
the biographer might consider to be of major import to the understanding
of his subject can be very different from how the individual would
regard the turn of events and the development of his life. With autobiography there will be the recall of what appears to be a terribly small
event—a word spoken, an interaction played out—that will appear to
have been a critical point. The selection of such events is ultimately
linked to the perspective of the individual at the time of the writing.
Had his view been different, another event might have been recalled
or significance appended. As Weintraub suggests, "A hallmark of autobiography is that it is written from a specific retrospective point of
view, the place at which the author stands in relation to his cumulative
experiences when he puts interpretative meaning on his past."[2] There
is then the image of the individual at a particular moment in his life
stopping and asking of himself what meaning this particular life has
at this moment and how this life has arrived at this juncture. In other
words, the individual states, as it were, let me look to my past, let me
see what meaning it possesses to help me understand myself today.

One might proceed in several ways with the task of summing up
one's life. At its most mundane level autobiography might be little more
than a statement of what the individual was in the past and what he
is today. That is, autobiography can be simply a recording of events
and circumstances with their intervening experiences and personalities
in which there is little or no attempt to draw the meaning of the self
away from the events experienced. The self is defined and interpreted
in terms of the experiences themselves, rather than defining itself in
relation to, or independent from, such experiences. In addition, meaning
may also be presented as a given, precisely in the concreteness of its
character, rather than as the adumbration of the mystery of its being
and process. As such, autobiography is not serious self-reflection, it is
a banal and vain show marked more by its hubris than its insight.

It is, as Pascal has noted, the character of truly significant autobiography, however, that the self appears not as a static given, not as
something molded by circumstances, but rather as an entity equally in
the process of unfolding and making the journey. As Pascal has said,
"the life is represented in autobiography not as something established
but as a process."[3] Thus we see within the very progression of the
autobiographical task a deep unfolding of the self. As such, autobiography
is not simply the narration of the journey, but it is the journey itself.

If the journey is the following of a map of a route already charted,
then the self is a tabloid already printed and read, and its record ferrets
out no new manifestations in the growth of the self. If, however, this

is a true journey, then each step taken charts the map for the first time and the actual meaning of the self may be said to emerge from incipiency to being within the act of charting the journey. As Weintraub has put it, true autobiography is "moved by a deeply felt need to understand the meaning of one's being and life. The sheer act of writing is thus an act of self-orientation."[4]

It has been said that autobiography combines self-questioning, self-discovery, and self-evaluation.[5] Self-questioning may be seen as an attempt to ask of the self the secrets of the self. Self-discovery suggests the perception of an order and pattern to the diversity and complexity of individual events and experiences. Self-evaluation points to the emergency of meaning in the perception of continuity and process. Thus the mark of true autobiography—self discovers self as it journeys into self, reading from its own tabloid its measured steps through time.

II

Taking ideas such as self-questioning, self-discovery, and self-evaluation as well as the entire framework of interpretation of autobiography as a journey in the discovery of the meaning of the self, how might we assess the autobiography of Mircea Eliade? As a genre, autobiography is immensely popular, yet few would regard the vast majority of autobiographical statements as genuinely probing the self and its journey to self-understanding. In the case of the autobiography of Eliade, however, there can be little doubt as to the genuineness of the task undertaken and the penetrating nature of the result accomplished. There remains as central to his autobiography a focus upon the self and its growth of meaning.

It has been interesting that in lengthy, personal conversations with Eliade on the nature and meaning of his autobiography and his sense of the importance of the undertaking of the autobiographical task, Eliade suggested a growth in his own self-understanding through the process of the autobiographical journey. Eliade said that when he first began his autobiography, it was with a sense of the importance of the events and the times his life had passed through and in turn been witness to. The feeling, as he described it to me, was that unless he was to record his own experiences, something of that time would be lost. Its events and personalities would slip into the realm of the historical, lacking any intimacy of personal recollection. He then had a sense of what we would refer to as the memoir. As a genre, the memoir focused upon the time and the people and events of the time described; what focus there was upon the individual was only in relation to the times themselves.

Would it be more appropriate to refer to Eliade's autobiography as a memoir? The answer is a resounding "no." The reason is that as Eliade continued to describe his own evolution of feeling toward the autobiography, he spoke of a change in his attitude toward what he was doing in the actual writing of the work. Although his initial intention was to record the times and the perspective of one in the Eastern European milieu, Eliade began to be fascinated with the recollection of the self within the memory of the times. As the process of the auto-biographical task unfolded completely, he began to discover the self in earnest—not simply static images of the self as so many photographs in a book, but the self in journey step by step unfolding its own many secrets.

He described it in this way: As the autobiography began to take shape and form a pattern before him, he realized that although the issue of recording a time and its events might have some value in itself, the value that was beginning to emerge in the autobiographical task was of a different order. He realized for the first time that as he engaged in the process of recollecting and recounting his life, he began to discover something about himself. Thus the writing of the autobiography took on the quality of self-discovery and ultimately the establishment of meaning for the self. What Eliade recounted of his feelings about the writing of the autobiography suggests precisely why the work goes far beyond the limits of the memoir and strikes at the very heart of the autobiographical task—the journeying into self.

In episode after episode recounted by Eliade of his early years, one can see the process of the journey unfolding and the struggle to establish meaning. Early in the autobiography, for example, Eliade discusses an early literary composition, "How I Found the Philosopher's Stone," written for a competition with a topic that was to be centered upon a scientific subject treated in a literary manner. He composed what he described as a brief fantasy concerning the discovery of the alchemist's "philosopher's stone." The reader is carried along by the fascinating transformation of raw materials into gold, only to find in the end that the entire tale had been a dream. There was no philosopher's stone, only the dream of it. What is the significance of this event? Why is this particular episode recounted and told? Eliade states, "I never reread that story, but when I thought about it, decades later, I realized that it was not without significance."[6] It was, in autobiographical perspective, the punctuation of a particular moment in which a fantasy of alchemy, or perhaps more meaningfully, a dream of alchemy, had emerged in a context of interest and knowledge of chemistry, at a time when there was yet no contact of any kind with the literature of alchemy. That was to come later in a level of such intensity that Eliade says, "Since then I have never lost interest in the subject."[7]

Thus a seemingly small episode bears meaning for a major interest of his life and by recollecting the episode there is a thread of meaning provided that permits understanding the emergence of later interests. Only by engaging in the conscious recollection of events and experiences of early life did this particular episode come to light—an episode easily lost in the sheer density of events that make up a life, yet with its recollection there is a step taken in probing the self. Here, after all, was concrete evidence that even at the point when the main focus was upon the study of natural science, and in particular chemistry, well before any intentional contact with that vast subject of alchemy, here in an essay written for a competition was a spark of an interest that in a sense explains itself by its own later development. If alchemy had never become an absorbing interest, then this essay would have had little significance in unraveling the mystery of the thread of continuity of the self. Such is the nature of autobiography that given the perspective of the time of writing—the sense of the self—the process of recollection orients itself to the reconstruction of the self's journey toward its present moment of self-understanding.

Another mark of autobiography is Eliade's acute awareness of the degree to which moments recalled but not entirely understood are not without significance to the entire journey of the life. Thus the observation, "But I am constrained to note here this . . . because, I suspect, it too has its meaning."[8] The marvel of this observation is the degree to which it focuses upon the act of self-discovery. It suggests, in its utter honesty, that even as this is recorded, its meaning has yet to be entirely manifest. Still, it is recorded with the spirit of journeying for meaning, recognizing that this too will play its part in the gradual emergence of meaning of the self. One can almost see the thought process going on in this passage. Something has been recalled, something that strikes a deep accord with the self-discovery, yet the manner in which it fits into the act of self-discovery is not yet entirely clear. While it is still unclear, there is something about this particular point that continues to demand to be remembered. Therefore record it, as one would other items, with the understanding that the meaning of self is unfolding in this entire process of recollection and recording. The pieces do not yet entirely fit into a total picture, but they are recorded with the assumption that they will fit and that the pattern and order and structure will become clear.

One of the central features of establishing meaning and self-under-standing in autobiography is to be able to chart a particular direction that may be seen as the thread connecting often remarkably differing events. This is not to suggest that a connection has always been there, even subconsciously, much less a clear direction established. In fact it is often the case that the autobiography will focus upon the transition from events with little or no order or meaning to the point at which the life takes on meaning and in which a clear pattern or direction has emerged. This is particularly the case with autobiographies that would be considered religious or philosophical in orientation. It is the founding of the religious or philosophical point of view that takes the life from a set of random experiences to one of order, pattern, and direction. This is, of course, still observed as is all autobiographical writing from the perspective at the time of writing and as such the point of first orientation will be viewed as a commencing of pattern and meaning to life, a process fulfilling itself in the autobiographical journey itself.

We have a wonderful example of this process in Eliade's autobiography. In his chapter entitled "The Temptations of the Nearsighted Adolescent," Eliade describes his melancholia, his lack of purpose, and the general feeling of sadness that pervaded his life. He describes this in the following way:

> The attacks of melancholia, with which I was to struggle for many years to come, had started. It required a great effort of will for me to resist the first outbreaks of sadness. . . . I felt there was no purpose in my life, that there was no reason for me to spend my time reading or writing. In fact, nothing held any meaning for me now; neither music, nor camping trips, nor walks, nor parties with my friends.[9]

As he describes his feeling with sensitive introspection, he identifies
at least part of the source of this sadness as his growing recognition
of his own maturing. The implication of the self-consciousness of his
maturation is that he senses that some things are now of the past and
not again to be experienced. And as some things are of the past, so
too the carefreeness of youth passes. It is a turning point, and one that
carries with it a pathos for the transition to be made and the life that
by such rites of passage is left behind. Here the sadness is seemingly
focused upon that which is left behind, but there is as well a sense of
the critical nature of the journey ahead, for what lies ahead are the
decisions concerning direction and focus that will chart the steps of the
life itself.

Thus in the chapter "Navigare Necesse Est . . ." we find the critical
resolve taking place that will begin to provide the direction for the
course of the life. The student who has specialized in natural sciences,
but who spends most of each night in literary pursuits, resolves to
move in the direction of the field for which he is primarily known
today.

> Little by little during the seventh year I found myself becoming estranged
> from my beloved natural sciences, physics, and chemistry, and increasingly
> fascinated not only by literature, which I had loved since childhood, but also
> by philosophy, Oriental Studies, and the history of religions.[10]

The decision to navigate had been made and for the first time a course
was set. This is not to suggest that there had not been plans and
decisions made before the crucial turning point, but simply that in
autobiographical perspective, this was the transition that emerged as of
paramount importance, for it was this transition and none before it that
steered Eliade's life in the direction it was to continue to chart—this
was the point at which the journey commenced.

That the journey has commenced does not also imply that this is
somehow the end of misgivings, doubts, or sadness. As Eliade states,
melancholia was something he struggled with for years, and certainly
in the potential nadir of feelings represented by that melancholia, there
would be little sense of a purpose providing a bright road to follow.
What then is the weight and the meaning of this transition that makes
it stand out as a turning point in the autobiography? The transition
implies most directly for Eliade a new direction taken, a facing up to
his actual interests and the making of a resolve to pursue these interests.
With hindsight, such a resolve stands out as a critical turning point,
and with that hindsight the sheer randomness of the daily events of
life take on direction and purpose. Again, however, this is a perspective

of looking back, it is not the coursing of the events of each day lived. When experienced within the context of each day, the thread of purpose becomes more and more difficult to see, let alone to follow. Melancholia is then an experience of the moment, a moment in which the sight of the thread has been lost. In autobiography the thread is seen with a clarity as if one was looking from a mountain peak down upon the torturous and lengthy path that has been taken step by slow step.

III

As important as this turning point is in Eliade's maturing process and in gaining an initial sense of purpose to the years of life that lay ahead of him, the events surrounding this transition pale when compared to his journey East, his trip in search of the meaning of India and equally in search of the meaning of himself.

India was for Eliade a pilgrimage; it stood as the logical conclusion to the turning point of his early years. Once his study of the natural sciences had been put aside, once he had turned to the serious study of history of religions and Oriental studies, the fascination with India could only result in the eventual journey to India. It was not simply travel but pilgrimage, for India was the great repository of all that Eliade held to be the focus of his studies—the subtlety of Eastern thought in its most pure and quintessential form lay as the very foundation of Mother India. As with any true pilgrimage, it was as much a journey into the self as a journey of the self.

In describing what was waiting for him in India Eliade says:

> It was there for me to decipher and . . . in deciphering it I would at the same time reveal to myself the mystery of my own existence; I would discover at last who I was and why I wanted to be what I wanted to be, why all things that had happened to me had happened to me . . .[11]

Thus India was to be the very ground of self-discovery. As he looked upon it, somehow locked in the study of the ancient systems of Indian thought was the sense of gaining insight into himself, of understanding perhaps for the first time the turn of events of his life that had brought him on this pilgrimage, that had refocused his educational and eventual vocational plans in a most profound reorientation of his life. Were these goals set too high? Was this simply the expression of romantic youth looking with wondering eyes upon new and sacred topographies? The answer appears to be an emphatic no, for as the full experience of India, an experience of different levels of India, permeated Eliade's thinking, he was deeply affected, if not transformed.

Eliade went to India to study Indian philosophy with Dasgupta, probably the world's leading scholar of the time in the study of the classical systems of Indian thought. As he recounts, however, conflict soon broke out between he and Dasgupta. He was requested to leave the Dasgupta household, and rather than returning to a simple apartment dwelling, Eliade went in search of an ashram, a refuge where the understanding of religion was to be based upon the experience of religion rather than the level of scholarly knowledge acquired. For Eliade this transition was of extraordinary magnitude. What was ultimately at stake in terms of the unfolding of the autobiographical journey was nothing short of the discovery of himself. He describes Dasgupta as "historical India" and says, "The historical India was forbidden to me, the road now was open to 'eternal' India."[12] At the outset he had traveled to India seemingly with the sole purpose of studying at length with Dasgupta and it was through his study with Dasgupta that the secrets of Indian thought were to become manifest. In the end, however, extraordinary events follow from what initially appears as a complete setback in the intended plans. Suddenly Dasgupta was, as Eliade says, forbidden. What then? What path was to be followed? The path that opened was the path to the center of India and in turn to the center of himself—the path that suggested that knowledge of religion was the experience of religion.

The experience of the ashram, as Eliade subtly observes, brought his understanding full circle to an insight that plays a central role in Eliade's sense of self.

> I realized also that I had to know passion, drama, and suffering before renouncing the "historical" dimension of my existence and making my way toward a trans-historical, atemporal, paradigmatic dimension in which tensions and conflicts would disappear of themselves.[13]

Here was the meeting of history and transcendence. Within the context of India it was Dasgupta who represented history and the practices of the ashram that represented its transcendence. The insight gained suggests not that one is to be condemned and the other venerated, but that both have their time and their place. Both play their role in the molding of the self, a self ultimately as much *of* history as *beyond* history. The autobiography can attribute this insight to the different levels of his experience in India. If India had only meant study with Dasgupta, there may have been little to sharpen the distinction of history and transcendence, let alone seeing the necessity of experiencing the self in both realms. Instead India was an education for Eliade, a tossing back and forth between the very distinctions that are the handiwork of the rational process and in the end to bring him to the experience of the many facets of the self, none more or less real than any other.

It was the journey East that brought these dimensions of the self into clear view and that suggested that all dimensions needed to be experienced, for anything less would only deny something of that strange bundle of components that bears the designation of self. In the end, however, it was the journey West that was to provide the full meaning to the self. In a fashion similar to experiencing both history and transcendence, the self was more than the product of a journey in only one direction. Self for Eliade is both a journey East and a journey West. This perception, however, matures only at the point of autobiographical perspective. It is more often the case that each stage of the journey seems to hold a quality of wholeness about it. But as in viewing the mountain path from the summit, a broader perspective does eventually distinguish between steps taken and the summit reached. In autobiographical perspective, the wholeness of the journey is not one direction, but both directions. The result is a delightful paradox for it is in journeying East and journeying West that the self has been centered.

IV

Ostensibly, the journey West for Eliade is the return from India to Europe and it is within this framework that the autobiography discusses it. In reality, however, the journey West is far more than simply the return from India. India, after all, had provided a context of self-discovery for Eliade, a self-discovery that did not fade away with the days of returning home to Europe. In fact, the process is really quite the reverse. The return home becomes in itself a further experience in self-understanding. Thus the journey West is an exploration of the meaning of the West and in particular Eliade's West, and its significance for his life. We find then in the final sections of the autobiography the capacity to see and experience the meaning of Romania and its significance for his own self-understanding. The perception of the meaning of Romania for Eliade was recognized as dependent upon the journey East itself. It was necessary to see India, or more, to experience India, and thus touch the roots of Indian spirituality in order to come to recognize his own roots sprung as they were from the soil of Romania. Eliade suggests the importance of the Indian experience in the following way:

Indirectly, the understanding of aboriginal Indian spirituality helped me, later on, to understand the structure of Romanian culture. . . . The most specific characteristics of Indian religiosity—above all, the cult of and the mystic devotion to goddesses of fertility—were the contribution of the aboriginal population or the result of a synthesis between autochthonous spirituality and that of the Indo-Aryans. I was to understand soon that the same synthesis had taken place in the history of Romanian culture.[14]

At one level these are the words of the historian of religions speaking, pointing to the synthesis of the Indo-Aryan world view and the elements of the autochthonous culture as the explanation of the full character of the world of Indian spirituality. It is still the historian of religions who notes with due interest that this same combination may be seen in the heritage of Romanian culture, thus noting the common modalities of the sacred and the potential commonality of structure in the religious world view of these historically diverse cultures. Yet there is more to this insight than simply the interest of the historian of religions, as interesting and insightful as that aspect of it might be, for this is an insight that bears directly upon the nature of self-discovery and self-understanding. This is an insight that suggests understanding of the very nature of the self. India has shown the diverse modalities of the sacred and the delicate balance with which they are held. The return to Romania has shown a common structure and thus the degree to which someone whose roots are in Romania would not only be sensitive to this structure, but in the end would see the very same structure operating within himself.

Here, then, is the completion of the journey, or at least this phase of the journey, for the East has been experienced and now the West is understood. At root, however, the issue remains the degree to which the self has come to understand its own meaning. Thus the journey East was essential, but so too the journey West. The self only emerges in the journeying that encompasses both East and West.

We find that as the autobiography draws to its conclusion there is also a conclusion as regards the self. The conclusion draws from the meaning of traveling both East and West to inform the sense of self and suggest that a glimmer of clarity of understanding exists. There are facets of the self and in the interplay of these facets, the self is neither one nor the other exclusively. Rather, the self is held in the interplay. A paradox? Perhaps. And appropriately so! Eliade says of himself that he lives paradoxically. He means by this that he lives both in history and beyond history. There is no resolution to this paradox but for the recognition of the ubiquitous nature of the realm of oppositions, *coincidentia oppositorum*, and thus the sense that at the base of every intrusion of the sacred into the world lies the paradox of the interplay of the finite and the infinite. To recognize the paradox is to see the meaning of the self, to accept the burden of history, or what has been called the terror of history, as a prelude to that which is beyond history. The recognition of that which is infinite, of that which is beyond history, is an insight by the individual for the self. It cannot be shared, for it must be experienced. It is of the nature of a secret, and yet the multitude demands historical vulnerability. The paradox of life continues, caught in history with glimpses beyond history, living in the interplay of eternity and ephemerality, journeying through the self to the realization of the self, establishing relative meaning but perceiving infinite value.

Notes

1. Roy Pascal, *Design and Truth in Autobiography* (Cambridge, Mass.: Harvard University Press, 1960), p. 9.

2. Karl Weintraub, *The Value of the Individual: Self and Circumstance in Autobiography* (Chicago: University of Chicago Press, 1978), p. xviii.

3. Pascal, p. 182.

4. Weintraub, p. 24.

5. Weintraub, p. 26.

6. Mircea Eliade, *Autobiography: Journey East, Journey West* (San Francisco: Harper & Row, 1981), p. 55.

7. Eliade, p. 56.

8. Eliade, p. 289.

9. Eliade, p. 72.

10. Eliade, p. 89.

11. Eliade, p. 153.

12. Eliade, p. 189.

13. Ibid.

14. Eliade, p. 203.

PART THREE

Souvenirs

DAVÍD CARRASCO

——————— §ß ———————

Mircea Eliade
and the "Duration of Life":
An Abundance of Souvenirs

Mircea Eliade was born in Bucharest, Romania, on March 9, 1907, and died in Chicago, Illinois, on April 22, 1986. But those of us who were his students, his friends, and his colleagues know it is erroneous to see those dates as the duration of his life and influence. For as Charles Long eloquently stated in his eulogy for Eliade last week in Chicago, "Mircea Eliade symbolized the excellence of the human mode of being." In fact, Eliade told us how to understand the duration of his life in a passage from his journal *No Souvenirs: Journal, 1957–1969*, in which he wrote in 1961:

Today, coming home from the university, in the vicinity of the Oriental Institute, I suddenly experienced my life's *duration*. Impossible to find just the right word. I suddenly felt, not older, but extraordinarily rich and full; expanded—bringing together in me, concomitantly both the Indian, Portuguese and Parisian "time" and the memories of my Bucharest childhood and youth. As if I had acquired a new dimension of depth. I was "larger," "rounder." An immense inner domain—where not so long ago, I was penetrating only fragmentarily by trying to relive such-and-such an event—was revealed in its totality: I'm able to see it from end to end and at the same time, in all its depth.

A vigorous, strong feeling. Historical human life suddenly takes on meaning and significance. Optimism.

In this passage about reminiscence and integration, optimism and life's

This lecture was delivered at the inauguration of the American Romanian Congress of Arts and Sciences, May 1986, University of Colorado at Boulder.

"roundness," we see reflected some of the major events, movements, and underlying characteristics of Mircea Eliade's life. In the time allotted to me I would like to weave together the mode of personal reminiscence with the mode of intellectual assessment as a way of illuminating some of the significance of his life and life's work. I realize, of course, that Eliade's worth has already been displayed in his life and deeds—he has already honored himself, and I don't wish to imperil that honor by reducing him to my vision, reminiscence, and evaluation. So I will enlarge upon the custom of eulogy by combining my memories of him with his own memories, as recorded in his writings, with the memories of others who have attempted to praise, understand, and evaluate his significance. For no one person or even group can adequately say what he did and what he has left us.

In 1966, when Professor Eliade received the doctor of humane letters at Yale University, the president of Yale, Kingman Brewster, read this citation:

> You belong to the world. In early youth you voyaged from Europe into the introspective wisdom of the East, and having probed the essence of Indian spirituality, you have worked to render the East more understandable to the West. Venerating the great mysteries expressed in myth and symbol, you have

helped to find the human language for eternal truth. Yale confers upon you the degree of doctor of humane letters.

The global dimensions of Eliade's superb achievement were reflected again last week in Paul Riceour's comment that "Mircea Eliade was a great thinker in any language, and he was a great writer in French." I remember my first startled awareness of Eliade's worldwide influence and attraction during the years when I served as his student secretary. On the first day that I arrived at his now famous (and burned out) office on the third floor of Meadville Seminary, I was presented with a series of letters from many places and kinds of people who had written him for favors, advice, or to extend invitations. There was an invitation to visit Australia, give lectures at the major universities, tour the aboriginal lands, and meet with tribal leaders. There was a letter from the *Encyclopædia Britannica* inviting him to write several major articles on the history of religions, a letter from a conscientious objector serving time in prison asking Eliade to please send him more of his books because they helped him cope with the weight of time, a letter from a playwright in France asking permission to dedicate his play to Eliade, a plea from a widow to help her understand the mystery of life after death, and a thirty-three-page handwritten letter from a man who was in the midst of a religious experience while listening to the soundtrack from the movie *King of Kings*, surrounded with pictures of gurus on the walls of his room! Eliade had a cultural reach I could not have dreamed of, and this was just the first day of the job! Later I could relate to that article in the *New York Times* about the Arizona hitchhiker who asked his driver where he was heading, and when the driver answered Chicago, the youth exclaimed, "Oh, that is where Mircea Eliade lives." As Kingman Brewster said, "He belonged to the world."

But we must remember that Eliade was formed and fashioned in Romania, and it was in his discoveries as a student in Romania that he found the possibilities to overcome provincialism and seek a wider understanding of humankind. He talks about his expansion of perspective in the book *Ordeal by Labyrinth*.

We were the first generation to receive our cultural education in what at that time was called "greater Romania"—the Romania that emerged from the 1914–18 war. The first generation without an already established program, without a ready-made ideal to turn into a reality. My father's generation and my grandfather's had been presented with an ideal already formed: the unification of all the Romanian provinces. That ideal was now realized. And I was lucky enough to be part of the first generation of Romanians to be *free*, to have no set *program*. We were free to explore not only the traditional sources of culture—in other words, the classics and French literature—but all the rest as well. I had discovered Italian literature, the history of religions, and the East. One of my friends had discovered American literature; another, Scandinavian culture. We discovered Milarepa, in the Jacques Bacot translation. Everything was possible, you see. We were getting ready for a real breakthrough at last.2

By the age of twenty-five, he had revealed to Romania and Eastern Europe an extraordinary scope of mind and spirit that was expressed in his writings on myths and symbols and initiatory structures of Oriental religion, and in his literary works, which bore such titles as *Isabel and the Devil's Waters, Soliloquies,* and *The Light That Failed.* But Eliade had realized that for him to make a real breakthrough he had to travel to India, an experience that set the pattern for a life of wanderings. In India his distinct genius was enhanced by his study of Sanskrit and Indian philosophy under Surendrenth Dasgupta and his initiation into Yogic techniques in the Himalayan ashram of Rishekesh under the guidance of Swami Shivananda. These experiences resulted in the classic study *Yoga: Immortality and Freedom,* which opened up to the West new ways of understanding the spiritual universe of India.

On a personal level, several traumatic experiences led him to an awakening of his destiny in life. He writes of this awakening in his *Autobiography: Journey East, Journey West:*

Neither the life of an "adopted Bengalese" nor that of a Himalayan hermit would have allowed me to fulfill the possibilities with which I had come into the world. Sooner or later I should have awakened from my "Indian existence"—historical or transhistorical—and it would have been difficult to return, because by that time I should not have been only twenty-three. What I had tried to do—renounce my Western culture and seek a "home" or a "world" in an exotic spiritual universe—was equivalent in a sense to a premature renunciation of all my creative potentialities. I could not have been creative except by remaining in *my* world—which in the first place was the world of Romanian language and culture. And I had no right to renounce it until I had done my duty to it: that is, until I had exhausted my creative potential. I should have the right to withdraw permanently to the Himalayas at the *end* of my cultural activities, but not at the beginning of them. To believe that I could, at twenty-three, sacrifice history and culture for "the Absolute" was further proof that I had not understood India. My vocation was culture, not sainthood. I ought to have known that I had no right to "skip steps" and renounce cultural creativity except in the case of a special vocation—which I did not have. But of course I understood all this only later . . .

One of the remarkable characteristics of Eliade's life was his movement—both geographical and intellectual—over the world. His movements from Romania to Lisbon, to Paris, and eventually to Chicago, where he founded the Journal of the History of Religions and became the Sewell L. Avery Distinguished Service Professor, was his way of deciphering and ordering the cosmos. But Eliade's movements across boundaries were not in the spirit of colonialism. It was his way of living within the historical situation of his time and undergoing periodic experiences of deprovincialization. His ability to undergo change through the encounter with the Other and others resulted in a creative hermeneutics that created major parts of an intellectual tradition called the history of religions. After he and Christinel moved to the University of Chicago when he was forty-nine, his voluminous writings continued to cover an astonishing breadth of topics from primitives to zen. His writings have been translated into thirteen languages, which carry the titles of such classics as *Patterns in Comparative Religions, The Myth of the Eternal Return, Shamanism: Archaic Techniques in Ecstasy, The Forbidden Forest, The Old Man and the Bureaucrats, Mephistopholes and the Androgeny,* and the monumental *History of Religious Ideas.* His extraordinary success at the University of Chicago resulted, earlier this year, in the establishment of the Mircea Eliade Chair in the History of Religions. At the celebration for this event, one scholar noted:

> There are many, many scholars, not only in Europe and North America, but in Australia, in Asia, in Africa, and in South America as well, who firmly believe that Mircea Eliade has been and remains, in the area of Religious Studies, and perhaps in the Humanities more generally, the most original, the most creative, and the most important scholar of his entire generation.

Two stories about Eliade demonstrate that this evaluation of his contribution was not an exaggeration. Jerald Brauer, former dean of the Divinity School at the University of Chicago, tells the story of how another university tried desperately to lure Eliade away. In 1965 four Albert Schweitzer chairs were founded in private and state universities in New York State. In an attempt to draw the greatest humanistic scholars to these chairs, Eliade was one of the first scholars wooed for a Schweitzer chair that involved twice the salary Eliade was receiving plus a $10,000 research fund and other support. Brauer recalls the day that Eliade informed him of his decision to stay at Chicago.

> One day Mircea was in my office discussing the situation of his journal, *The History of Religions.* During the conversation he very nonchalantly stated that I probably heard he had received an offer for a Schweitzer chair. My heart virtually stood still as I replied that I had. Before I could say another word, he indicated that he was not interested in the Schweitzer chair, and that he was determined to stay at the Divinity School. Eliade very quietly said, "Is there any reason why I should leave? I came here to establish the discipline of the History of Religions, and we are well on the way. I have my journal, I have my students, I have my colleagues, I have the University, and we have our friends here in Chicago. Why should I leave?"

There was one occasion when the University of Chicago and the United

States almost lost Eliade to Europe. Due to a visa mix-up, it appeared that the Eliade's would have to live outside the United States for a minimum period of two years before they would be permitted reentry unless it could be demonstrated that Eliade's work was indispensable to the security and welfare of the United States. Such exceptions were sometimes made, but always for scientists working with weapons and military purposes. During the process of making this argument, a woman at the Department of Defense responsible for analyzing dossiers and writing waiver requests telephoned the administration at the University of Chicago. She said that in all her years of examining dossiers from individuals who claimed their work was indispensable to the security and welfare of the United States, Eliade was the "first individual who was truly needed for the welfare of the U.S." He possessed the kind of knowledge, interests, and humanity that the nation so desperately required. The Defense Department, through the influence of the Assistant Secretary of Defense under President Eisenhower, James H. Douglas (friend of the Divinity School), agreed with the woman's assessment, and Eliade was granted immigrant status in 1961.

While Eliade had scores of students and colleagues, no one understood him better than Charles H. Long who delivered the "Eulogy for Mircea Eliade" at a memorial service held at Rockefeller Memorial Chapel on April 28. Long said:

> There has been a great deal of commentary and debate about the historical dimensions of Eliade's work. So much so, that one has the sense that he ignored ordinary, mundane modes of human existence. This is not so. He was an intellectual activist in Romania and associated with some of the most radical thinkers and artists in Paris. What is overlooked is his concern for human freedom and creativity and his sense that such modes of being cannot always be encompassed within the orders given by modern society and the modern state. For that matter all religious innovation from primitives to zen was inspired by a religious imagination that sought a deeper and more decisive statement of the human mode of being. It all depends on what you mean by freedom and how you define human existence. He wanted us to know that there are other questions, other nuances, other resolutions to these basic issues of our existence. And these questions, nuances and resolutions are not only present in the great systems of India and Chinese thought but also among the primitives in our own traditions and that they may be present today in the experience and expressions of our friends, neighbors and compatriots. It was this discernment and deciphering of human existence that was to the fore. A seriousness about the human matter that made him doubt the ready solutions of the mundane makers of history.

In 1974, Mircea Eliade autographed his book *Two Tales of the Occult* for me. The inscription read, "For Davíd Carrasco, these souvenirs from his student life in Swift Hall . . . these Two Tales of the Occult from Mircea

Eliade." I was immediately puzzled by his use of the word souvenir for I had come to associate the word with trinkets and sometimes gaudy reminders of a day at the circus, carnival, or a big city amusement park. But knowing that Eliade used words carefully and intentionally I looked up the word souvenir and was delighted to see that it combined the meaning "something serving as a token of remembrance of a place, occasion or experience" with the meaning "something which comes to one's aid." Some years later, when his journal *No Souvenirs* was published, with its title lamenting his having no momentos from Romania to aid him in Chicago, I came to understand how important the word was to him. And now we are in the fortunate position of having an abundance of souvenirs that he has left us, in his books, in his lectures, in our friendship with him.

When Mircea Eliade lay dying in the Mitchell Hospital two weeks ago, I had what psychoanalysts would call a fantasy about his experience of death. I imagined him lying on his deathbed—still, pale, quiet, alone—but at a private level of his mind and spirit—aware and observant of his own descent into death. I imagined and wished that he was alert and watching, with inner eyes, the passage from life into death into some form of rebirth. I imagined him practicing—even at the end—a creative hermeneutics of his own end, "acquiring a new dimension of depth, . . . seeing life from end to end." I wished that he was grappling with the drama and crisis of what he called, in *The Secret of Dr. Honigberger*, "the beginning of a new spiritual existence."

When I drew myself out of this fantasy and inquired why I had produced it, I remembered a dazzling afternoon a group of scholars from the Department of Religious Studies at the University of Colorado and The Naropa Institute spent with him during his visit to Colorado in 1982. Eliade's former student Reginald Ray had arranged an afternoon discussion at Naropa. We were sitting in an oval arrangement with Professor Eliade by the southern window through which bright sunlight was shining. He was smoking his pipe, and the light gave the smoke a purple aura. Seated next to him, I noticed that the sunlight created a bright purple glow, the shape of a galaxy, in the corner of his glasses. The discussion developed around the pattern of beatific visions that patients who have died and come back to life report. Eliade became animated at the discussion of this phenomenon, and after a series of stunning insights remarked, "What is meaningful is not whether these visions are about going to heaven or not, but that the human mind creates such wonderful images at the moment of death." I realized, with the help of this memory, this souvenir, the meaning of my fantasy. I desired that my teacher and friend have such a beatific experience at the hours of his death.

As Charles Long stated in Chicago last week, "Mircea Eliade is no longer with us. But those of us who knew him well imagine that he is somewhere near Rishekesh—ready to undergo yet another initiation. He lives among us in all communities where *homo religiosus* is a fundamental meaning of the human condition." So we are left with an abundance of souvenirs, which even his death cannot take away. He has left us souvenirs that are permanent and secure and of a nature expressed in a pagan song of deep lament, which many of us could recite:

> They told me, Heraclitus, they told me
>   you were dead;
> They brought me bitter news to hear and
>   bitter tears to shed.
> I wept as I remembered how often you and I
> Had tired the sun with talking and
>   sent him down the sky.
> And now that thou art lying, my dear old
>   Carian guest,
> A handful of grey ashes, long, long ago
>   at rest,
> Still are thy pleasant voices, they
>   nightingales, awake;
> For Death, he taketh all away, but them
>   he cannot take.

May 1986

JANE MARIE LAW

—————§♭—————

Renewed Reflections

Nearly nine years ago Mircea Eliade delivered what was to become one of his last major addresses to the academic community, his lecture "Waiting for the Dawn" in the Glenn Miller Ballroom at the University of Colorado. Now, nine years after the lecture, eight years after Eliade and I selected the fragments from his work for this anthology, and nearly six years after his death, I have the opportunity to scrutinize again the contents of this small volume, intended then, and intended now, as a tribute to the scope of vision and humaneness of purpose of our mentor and friend.

Clearly, an anthology is both more and less than the sum of its parts. The selections in this volume, when read together as one book, take on a different tone than if read in the published contexts in which they originally appeared. Quite simply, our controlling idea in choosing these selections was that the works included be in some way representative of Eliade's work as a whole. When he and I met to determine the selections for this volume, he was excited by the prospect of an anthology that would include not only what he termed his "diurnal," rational mode of scholarship, and his "nocturnal," mythological mode of literary creativity, but also selections from his autobiographical reflections. In this volume, we made an effort to include selections that showed Eliade reflecting on the very nature of his genius, what I then termed "the grand oscillation" between his different modes of creativity and self-reflection. The term "oscillation" points to the movement among the voices and hues of insight that constitutes the rareness of Eliade's brilliance.

The selections from Eliade's academic writings include his reflections on the apocalyptic visions of the early eighties (certainly still reverberating today), the emergence of a global perspective in culture, and his views at eighty years of age of the religious structures inherent in a "rediscovery" of shamanism by artists and young people in the 1960s and early 1970s.

147

These selections present his vision of the History of Religions as a discipline with the potential for becoming a new humanism, a vision that many of us, openly or secretly, still return to when we ask ourselves what we are really doing as historians of religions. Also included is his powerful critique of "historical man" from the perspective he so powerfully called "the terror of history."

For many academic writers who also write literature, one mode tends to become a mere didactic echo of the other. In Eliade's literary works, however, we see a distinct notion of narrative that, though resonating with the themes of his scholarly works, stands very much as an autonomous and alternative mode of reflection. Eliade wrote about the relationship between these two modes of work in an essay included in this volume entitled "Literary Imagination and Religious Structure." We also chose to include his comments on *fantastic literature*, the genre of much of his creative writing. From his literary works, ranging from short stories and novellas to the magnum opus of *The Forbidden Forest*, we tried to present selections showing the range of styles Eliade worked within and the themes and narrative structures he explored. At that time, we were limited by the availability of his literary works in English, and drew selections only from those works already in translation. In this present volume, however, we are fortunate to be able to include a heretofore unpublished piece of his literature entitled "In the Shadow of the Lily."

For the selections from Eliade's autobiographical works, we isolated what seemed to be representative issues from his remarkable life. They reflect his precocious career as an observer of the phenomenal world, as shown in the selection here entitled, "From Silkworms to Alchemy," his awareness at the age of twenty-three of the cultural context of his work, and his involvement with a remarkable group of young Romanian scholars from both Christian and Jewish backgrounds in a vital study group—the Criterion Group—which dealt with pressing intellectual movements of his day. These movements, incidentally, still dominate our intellectual imagination now: psychoanalysis, the early voices of critical ideology, the problem of bigotry, and the relationship between the languages of the sciences and the humanities.

The selections here, fragments of a much greater and unified life work, are intended to reveal some of the sparkle, warmth, and optimism that was Mircea Eliade. We hope this volume pays proper tribute to the brilliance of his life.

Ithaca, New York
February 1991

MAC LINSCOTT RICKETTS

─────── ◊ ♭ ───────

Introduction to
"In the Shadow of a Lily"

The novella "In the Shadow or Shade of a Lily" is the last work of fiction
Eliade is known to have written. He makes three brief references to it in
his published journal excerpts for 1982. On April 22 he speaks of beginning
the story, having written some twenty pages that day; at this time he
planned to call it "Exile." He was in Chicago and three days earlier
Christinel had undergone a major operation at the University of Chicago's
Billings Hospital. The doctors had given Eliade a favorable report and a
hopeful prognosis.[1] The novella was finished that summer at Egyalieres,
France, where Mircea and Christinel were vacationing. In the journal entry
for August 1 Eliade notes that he resumed work on the novella, now called
"La umbra unui crin," its definitive title. In the next day's entry he says that
Christinel read the story and didn't especially like it, so he added six more
pages and believes it is finished.[2] It was in October of that year that the
Eliades came to Boulder for the occasion that is the subject of this book.
     The novella is in the fantastic genre to which Eliade was strongly drawn,
especially in his later years. The fantastic element in this narrative is the
disappearance of certain heavily loaded trucks after midnight at a particular curve on a highway outside Paris. Readers familiar with Eliade's great
novel, *The Forbidden Forest,* will recall the key role played by disappearing
automobiles in that book; and in the novella, "Nineteen Roses" (published
in *Youth Without Youth and Other Novellas,* Ohio State University Press,
1988), a sleigh vanishes. In all these instances, the disappearing convey-
ances function as "vehicles of transcendence," as means of crossing from
this plane to another; and for those who know how to see them, they are
"signs" of and from a plane of reality that is higher and better than the one

we inhabit. In this novella, and in others he wrote, especially in the last twenty years or so of his life, Eliade shows us, as plainly as he wished to reveal them, his personal faith and hope.

Notes

1. Mircea Eliade, *Mircea Eliade: Journal IV, 1979–1985* (Chicago: The University of Chicago Press, 1990), pp. 62–63.

2. Ibid., p. 65.

MIRCEA ELIADE

In the Shadow of a Lily

He had barely taken his finger off the button when the door opened
suddenly, with a squeak. He realized he was holding up the bottle of wine
threateningly, as if to defend himself, and he blushed.

"Don't you know me anymore?" he asked, somehow managing to smile.
The other man stared at him suspiciously, frowning, not trying to hide his
irritation.

"I'm Postăvaru, Ionel Postăvaru. We were classmates at Liceul Sfântul
Sava."

And because the other man only shrugged, he asked him: "Aren't you
the attorney Enache Mărgărit, from Bucharest?"

"Yes, I am."

"Well, then, we were classmates in the first four years of lycée. At Sfântul
Sava!"

Mărgărit smiled melancholically and shrugged his shoulders again.
"That was a long time ago," he said.

"A very long time! Forty-eight years. But we met once since then, in
Bucharest, on the eve of the war. I can even tell you the date: March 1939.
We met on the Boulevard, in front of the bookstore Cartea Românească."

"I'm awfully sorry," Mărgărit interrupted him. "I don't remember now.
. . ." He pronounced the words slowly, as though it were an effort for him
to speak.

"Forgive me for insisting," Postăvaru began again after a few moments'
hesitation. "I realize you're busy. . . ."

"I'm expecting a friend," Mărgărit interrupted again. "When I heard the
doorbell, I thought it was he. And that surprised me, because ordinarily
he's late."

Postăvaru took out his handkerchief shyly and wiped his forehead.

Translated from Romanian by Mac Linscott Ricketts.

152

"Again, I beg your pardon. But it's about something very important. Very important for me, I mean. Only yesterday did I learn your new address. And tomorrow morning I have to leave, and I don't know when I'll have occasion to stop in Paris again. . . . It's something very important. And it won't take more than five or six minutes—ten at the most. . . . I've brought you some wine," he added, thrusting the bottle toward him awkwardly. "They assured me it was the very best they had. I didn't like the paper they wrapped it in, so I wadded it up and left it in the taxi."

"Thanks, but you shouldn't have gone to so much trouble. Come in, please. As you can see, things are in a mess. I've just moved in."

He set the bottle down on a shelf, absently, but catching sight of the label he picked it up again with both hands and examined it in amazement.

"But this is too much!" he exclaimed in a whisper. "This bottle cost you a fortune!"

"Think nothing of it," Postăvaru interrupted him. "I said to myself, we must celebrate our reunion in Paris. We've known each other for forty-eight years. And, I repeat, for me it's very important. There's something I want to ask you."

He sat down on the couch and pulled out his handkerchief again.

"Ask," Mărgărit encouraged him, drawing up a chair. "But I warn you, I don't have much news. I fled the country nine years ago. Things have changed a great deal since then. I'm sorry . . ."

"I know, I know," sighed Postăvaru. "But I want to ask you something, something having to do with the last time we met, in March of 1939. When I recognized you then, you were in a very heated discussion with a friend in front of the bookstore Cartea Românească, and I approached you and shook your hand. I saw you another time too, but I didn't dare speak to you then, either because you were surrounded by people who intimidated me, or else because I was in too much of a hurry . . ."

He broke off abruptly and folding his handkerchief he replaced it unhurriedly in his pocket.

"Don't smile," he began again after a pause, "but I assure you that those few words, that phrase your friend said then—I never knew his name, but I know he was your friend, and maybe he still is, if he's living yet. . . . Although, it's been almost thirty-five years since then. There was the war, and then all that came afterward."

"I don't exactly understand," said Mărgărit. "I don't see what you're driving at."

Postăvaru looked at him directly again, shyly, and tried to smile.

"I'm sorry; it's my fault. I've been riding all morning and now I'm rather tired. And I confess, expecting your friend to arrive at any minute, I don't know how to begin in order to be able to say it all, and say it quickly."

Mărgărit smiled. "Don't be alarmed; he's a good friend. A Romanian refugee, also. If he comes and you want to talk with me in private, I'll ask him to wait in the other room."

"No! He can stay. You'll see; there's nothing secret about it. But now that you've reassured me, may I ask you something else? Perhaps you have a bottle of beer handy, cold. I'm awfully thirsty. My mouth is dry."

Mărgărit got up and headed silently for the kitchen. He returned promptly with a bottle of beer and a glass, both of which he placed with exaggerated, ironic politeness on the little table in front of the couch.

"Nothing simpler!" he said, about to fill the glass.

But Postăvaru caught hold of his arm, smiling awkwardly.

"I heard you! You just now took it out of the refrigerator. It's too cold; it won't make a head. We must let it stand a little, to make it come to life! As our chemistry professor used to say—Vasile Safirim—you remember him don't you?—as Safirim used to say, 'Everything around us can freeze, even beer.' "

Mărgărit took a step backward, surprised, even startled, and stared at him curiously, as though he had just then realized who his guest was.

"Ah, yes, Vasile Safirim! I was walking through the Belu Cemetery once. It was a beautiful fall day. I remember it very well. I stopped to light a cigarette—in those days I smoked a lot—and when I flipped the match away I caught sight of a fresh grave, covered with flowers. And I read, 'Professor Vasile Safirim, 1880–1943.' Poor man! That was the first and last time I saw his grave. A little while later the American air raids occurred, and that part of the cemetery was blown up. You remember . . ."

"Poor Safirim! He was a great savant. He said to us, 'Everything around us can freeze.' He was thinking, of course, of the cold of the ground. But to keep from frightening us he added, in jest, 'even beer.' "

He picked up the bottle and held it in his hands for a few moments.

"Now, yes, I can pour. You'll see how the foam rises. Watch!"

Mărgărit shifted his position noisily in the chair.

"Well, and who was this friend of mine? I mean, what did he look like? Blond, brunette, tall, well-dressed?"

"I can't remember," Postăvaru admitted, "because, I repeat, that was the last time we ever met, in March 1939. It was on the Boulevard, in front of the bookstore Cartea Românesca. You were both talking at the same time, heatedly, as though you were about to quarrel. Your friend . . ."

"But what did he look like? Was he young, like us, or old?"

"He seemed about our age. He was wearing a hat with a narrow brim, pushed a little to the back of his head, and when he spoke, he gesticulated in a strange way."

"How do you mean?"

"I don't know how to explain it. He kept raising his arms as if he wanted to run his fingers through his hair, but he couldn't, because he had a hat on, you see. And then he didn't know what to do with his hands, so he stuck them quickly into his overcoat pockets. But is was obvious he was upset. He kept raising his voice higher and higher. Don't you remember now who he was?"

"No. A hat with a narrow brim . . ."

"But what he said was interesting," Postăvaru continued. "I repeat, you were both irritated, ready to quarrel. From what I could gather, you were trying to persuade him to make up with some mutual friend of yours. I never understood what the quarrel between *them* was about, because neither of you made any direct reference to it. But I was profoundly impressed by what he said. I'd never heard anything like it. Those words, I mean, or more precisely the philosophical concept—or perhaps it was even a mystical one—which he expressed suddenly, without any preliminaries . . ."

"But what did he say?!" Mărgărit broke in, scarcely controlling his impatience.

Postăvaru picked up the bottle of beer, then changed his mind abruptly and set it down again on the tray.

"He said—but wait, I have to add one detail. In exasperation, you asked him whether or not he'd decided to make up with your mutual friend, the one with whom he had quarreled. He looked at you very deeply, with sadness—and yet he smiled. It seemed to me a sarcastic smile. 'Oh, yes,' he said. 'I'll make up with him in the shadow of a lily in Paradise!' Notice: *in the shadow of a lily.*"

"Strange, I don't remember the conversation at all. You say he was about our age and had a hat with a narrow brim . . ."

"And he gesticulated constantly," Postăvaru added, talking faster and faster. "And he stuck his hands in his coat pockets, apparently in exasperation because he couldn't run them through his hair. Please, make an effort to remember! March 1939. In front of the bookstore Cartea Româneasca. After he left, we walked a few steps together, but not many, because you were angry and had no desire to talk. You never suspected how much those words impressed me: that he would be reconciled with that friend *in the shadow of a lily in Paradise!* And later they began to obsess me. Yes, to obsess me! After I was wounded at the Dniester Crossing. More precisely, shortly after I'd fallen, riddled with machine gun bullets, and I came to for just a moment or so with my face in the mud on the shoulder of the road. Since then, I haven't been able to forget them. And every time I've passed through a dangerous situation—and, like everyone else, I've been through many— your friend with the narrow-brimmed hat has come into my mind again, and I've heard him say: 'Oh, yes, in the shadow of a lily in Paradise' "

Mărgărit turned his chair around and drew it closer to the couch.

"It's exasperating!" he exclaimed. "It's exasperating that I could forget."

"Please, I beg of you!" insisted Postăvaru. "Make an effort to remember! You have no idea what this means to me. Maybe it will come to you later, after I go. I'll leave you my telephone number at the hotel, and my address in Zurich. Call me any time, any time at all. It's very important!"

Mărgărit listened to him absently, passing his right hand over first one knee, then the other.

"But actually," he burst out suddenly, "I don't really see in what sense I could help you."

"If you can remember who it was, you'll remember this detail also: if he and the friend ever made up, if they're still alive, and anything else you know about them. It's very important for me!" he repeated emotionally.

Just then Mărgărit heard footsteps approaching the door, and he rose to open it.

"Thank God you've come!" he said under his breath.

Postăvaru rose timidly from the couch and stepped to the middle of the room.

"Domnul* Eftimie, the friend I was expecting," Mărgărit presented him. "And this is domnul Ionel Postăvaru, a classmate of mine from Sfântul Sava," he added, smiling.

Eftimie shook his hand, looking him in the eyes almost severely.

"I'm glad to meet you," he said, taking a seat in the armchair to which Mârgârit had pointed. "I see you like the sofa," he continued, again looking him in the eyes enigmatically.

"This is where our friend, the host, seated me," Postăvaru started to explain, smiling. "In fact . . ."

"From Sfântul Sava, you say," Eftimie interrupted. "What a school!" he exclaimed, settling himself more comfortably in the chair. "It all started there, at Sfântul Sava. I was just talking with Dr. Tăusan. 'Really,' I said to him, 'what possessed you to tell those boys—mere children, fourteen to fifteen—to tell them about that business of the shadow of the lily in Paradise?' Because, it all started there . . ."

Postăvaru realized suddenly that he was blushing, and he reached for his handkerchief. He heard Mărgărit trying in vain to laugh sarcastically, but he didn't dare look at him.

"I didn't know," Mărgărit began, emphasizing each word, "I didn't know that you were in the habit of listening at the keyhole before ringing the doorbell!"

"What do you mean?" Eftimie replied calmly. "Who's been listening at the keyhole?"

"The matter of the shadow of a lily in Paradise."

"That's something I said to Dr. Tăusan, waiting for the metro. And we agreed: it was a foolish thing for him to say."

Postăvaru shot a glance at Mărgărit, then stood up suddenly.

"Pardon me!" he began. "Pardon me for interrupting. But I confess that

---

*Mister

I, like Mărgărit, can hardly believe you. Because, as Mărgărit will confirm, I came to see him—and I hadn't seen him since March of 1939—I came to see him precisely on account of that phrase, 'In the shadow of a lily in Paradise.' "

"Yes, yes," Eftimie interjected, "the phrase the professor spoke to the boys in Sfântul Sava."

"No, no," Mărgărit said, becoming irritated. "Don't mix things up. We, Postăvaru and I, were classmates at Sfântul Sava . . ."

"Forty-eight years ago," Postăvaru specified.

"But the story with the shadow of the lily in Paradise took place later."

"In March 1939."

"The story with the shadow of the lily has nothing to do with Sfântul Sava—at least, the Sfântul Sava of our adolescence."

He stopped, exhausted, and sat down again in his chair.

"I'll tell you what I said to Dr. Tăusan," Eftimie began again calmly. "This happened after our meeting—the meeting of our group—at the Café Excelsior. I'm sorry you weren't there too, Enache, because things have become complicated." He lowered his voice. "And there could be consequences for us all—us Romanians in exile, I mean."

Mărgărit sprang to his feet. "I feel as though I'm going to lose my mind and start screaming! What's it all about?"

Eftimie regarded him a few moments in bewilderment; then his face brightened. "I'm sorry," he said. "I thought you knew. I'd forgotten you weren't at church last Sunday."

"I was in the country. On account of *them* again. The same old thing. Always, the same old thing!"

"Now I remember. Well, briefly, we met according to agreement at the Excelsior, to see what we could do to help Iliescu."

"What's happened to him?" Mărgărit interrupted.

"You'll find out directly. But tell me first if you know Iliescu, the engineer."

"Not personally, but I know who he is, of course. I read about him in the papers, how he managed to make it to Vienna hidden for *five days* in a trunk."

"It was even more extraordinary than that! I'll tell you the whole story some day."

"But what's happened to him?" Mărgărit insisted.

"I'll tell you what Iliescu told me. Imagine—he's been transferred from Briançon and still he hasn't been told what department he'll be assigned to. For the time being, he is, as he says, 'on vacation.' More seriously, he's become suspect. He senses—or, rather, he *knows*—that he's being followed. And all this just because he told some of his colleagues what he found out from Valentin!"

"Hold on," Mărgărit interrupted, leaning on the back of the chair. "I don't exactly understand what this is all about."

"But I haven't finished!"

"I know, I know you have more to say. But before you go on, I want to ask what you'd like to drink: coffee, orange juice, wine?"

"At this time of day, I'd say wine."

Mărgărit started toward the kitchen somewhat gravely. "And I'll bring *you* another bottle of beer," he said over his shoulder to Postăvaru, smiling.

The longer the silence lasted, the more Postăvaru felt the severe looks of the other man.

"The same phrase!" he murmured. "There are tens, perhaps hundreds of thousands of Romanians in exile, scattered over the face of the earth, and it happens that today, of all days, while I'm passing through Paris to seek out Mărgărit, to ask him about a phrase I heard in 1939, you come in, and no sooner have you entered than you utter the *same phrase*. What a coincidence!"

"If you meet Iliescu, don't talk to him about coincidences. For him, a mathematician and specialist in statistics, the most extraordinary coincidences are as natural as the rule of three."

"Mathematically he might be right, but . . ."

He interrupted himself in order to help Mărgărit to set the tray of refreshments on the little table.

"I see you're spoiling me," said Eftimie, lifting his glass and holding it ceremoniously in his right hand.

"Mathematically, I say," Postăvaru resumed, "he might be right; and yet—*the same phrase!*"

"But it wasn't *his* phrase," Eftimie pointed out, smiling mysteriously. Then, after taking a sip of the wine, he added, "Excellent! I repeat, you're spoiling me!"

Mărgărit drew up the chair again and sat down. Then, with a sudden gesture, he took a pack of "Gauloises" out of his pocket.

"It's my first cigarette today," he explained, a little chagrined. "In fact, I don't smoke any more. But I always keep a pack handy. When I feel too nervous, I light up. Last Sunday," he said, addressing Eftimie, "I smoked almost a whole pack!"

"That was a bad thing to do," Eftimie replied. "You'd have done better to have stayed in Paris and met Iliescu—so you'd know what to expect!"

"But why? Why?" asked Mărgărit, exasperated.

"We'll talk of this later. But please, don't interrupt me. I'll start from the beginning, that is, from two years ago when Iliescu took Valentin Iconaru under his wing. You know, Iliescu works at the Center for the Supervision of Motor Vehicles, and for several years he's lived in Briançon. He has a big house, even though he's a bachelor, so when he met Valentin he invited him to come live with him, as a kind of secretary. I don't know him, but according to Iliescu's description and those of other Romanians who have visited him in Briançon, this Valentin was twenty-five or twenty-six and didn't seem too bright. He didn't learn to speak French very well, although he knew how to read it, and he read constantly. But he read only about animals and insects—especially insects. And when he spoke, which was seldom, he would talk about nothing but animals and insects. Iliescu couldn't depend on him, because he would disappear from the shop or the office, and when he would reappear—sometimes after two or three days— he always had the same excuse: that he had been chasing a butterfly, or a beetle, or whatever, and had gotten lost in the mountains."

"He ought to have given him a lecture, and then sent him back to Paris, to let him see what the exile means!" Mărgărit exploded.

"Iliescu has a heart of gold," Eftimie went on, after filling his glass. "And he admitted to us that, crazy as the young man was, he had been interested in him from the beginning, from the evening when he had spoken to him about how Fabre's *Souvenirs entomologiques* ought to be rewritten today. But, as I told you, everything started with a seemingly banal event. About two months ago, the two of them were resting on a large rock in the full sunlight and he, Valentin, caught a blue lizard and held it in his palm, staring at it as if he couldn't get enough of it. And all at once he heard him say, talking mostly to himself: 'When we all get to Paradise, in the shadow of a lily, I'll understand what this lizard is saying to me now.' Iliescu looked at him curiously and asked him, as a joke: 'But how do you know that lilies grow tall in Paradise?' The young man smiled, without looking up. 'This was something a professor at Sfântul Sava told us. Actually, he wasn't a teacher by profession, but he had changed his name and had obtained false papers. He was discovered by the Securitate and arrested.' "

Mărgărit jumped up from his chair and put his hand on his forehead. "Of course!" he exclaimed. "It was he! Flondor. Emanoil Flondor, the architect. How could I have failed to remember? With the narrow-brimmed hat. At that time, that spring, he wore a hat. Soon after that he gave it up and from then on he went bareheaded."

Postăvaru crossed himself and, very moved, rose to his feet. "Thank God you've remembered! And did they make up? This is what I came for," he added, taking a step toward Eftimie. "To find out if he ever made up with his friend."

"With Sandy Valaori, the newspaperman. They were good friends, and they had quarreled over some trifle. But eventually they were reconciled. They even decided to have a party, just the two of them, at their favorite tavern, as soon as the war would end. But they never did it. Sandy was implicated in the Maniu trial and was given twenty-five years at hard labor. Then Flondor disappeared, changed his name, somehow obtained a diploma and false papers, and became a professor of history, first at a gymnasium in the provinces and then at Bucharest, to replace a faculty member at Sfântul Sava who had been killed in an auto accident. But after five or six months he was arrested—apparently someone denounced him—and he was sentenced to fifteen years."

"But do you know anything else about them? Are they still alive?"

Mărgărit sat down absently on the chair and sought his pack of cigarettes again.

"I heard that Sandy Valaori had died after a few years in prison. At any rate, I never saw him again. As for Flondor, I know nothing precise. Some say he too died, without specifying when or in what circumstances."

Eftimie did not try to hide his irritation at having been interrupted, but on hearing Mărgărit's last words, he turned his head quickly.

"Others say he escaped and crossed the border, but again, it isn't known when or how."

"This is something Iliescu can tell you about," Eftimie intervened. "That is, not he, but Valentin, the young man we were speaking of a little while ago. Valentin claims that your man is alive, that he has seen him several times, that they've even spoken with each other."

"Extraordinary!" exclaimed Mărgărit in a whisper.

"But he," continued Eftimie, "Valentin, won't tell anyone how they met or what they talked about, because he says no one would believe him."

"What does he mean by that?" asked Mărgărit, rubbing his forehead. "I don't understand."

"I'm not sure I understand what he means myself, because I was told all this by Iliescu, and since there was so much to tell, he didn't have time to go into details. In any event, Iliescu is an engineer, a man with both feet on the ground, and he doesn't let himself be taken in by illusions, visions, or whatever. And when Valentin confided to him one day that after midnight *certain trucks disappear* as soon as they pass a curve at a specific location on the highway, Iliescu smiled. 'Very interesting,' he said to him. 'I want to see them disappearing at the curve for myself. But how will I know if they disappear or not? I'll have to take Marc along too [Marc is his co-worker, a man he trusts], and we'll keep watch, ten or fifteen meters apart, on either side of the curve.' And so they did. A little before midnight they 'camouflaged' themselves (as he put it) behind the trees, and whenever a truck would approach, Iliescu would whistle, imitating the call of some nocturnal bird."

Eftimie reached out, picked up the glass, and before lifting it to his lips added: "All three of them had learned long before this how to imitate the short, shrill whistle of that nocturnal bird." Then he sipped his drink slowly and sought a more comfortable position in the armchair.

"For the first two hours everything went normally. But suddenly there appeared a truck, heavily loaded yet traveling exceptionally fast. And ten or fifteen seconds after he had signaled, Iliescu heard Marc's whistle, indicating that the truck had *not* passed him. Iliescu ran to check. Indeed, on the highway that made a gradual ascent through the forest immediately beyond the turn, no trace of the vehicle could be seen. Only far away, much higher up, they could distinguish through the trees the lights of the truck that had preceded the other by five or six minutes."

"Extraordinary!" whispered Mărgărit.

"We said the same thing when we heard it," continued Eftimie. "But Iliescu is a man of science. When Valentin asked him, 'Do you agree that I was right?' he answered calmly, 'For the time being it's impossible to draw any conclusions. Let's see what will happen.' And the two men switched positions. Iliescu camouflaged himself in a thicket directly opposite the turn, and Valentin gave the same signal to announce the approach of each truck. And that night, Iliescu told us, *three more* trucks disappeared. 'Now you must be convinced!' Valentin insisted. 'Convinced I wasn't lying!' 'But I still haven't seen your professor from the Sfântul Sava,' Iliescu countered. 'And until I do see him, I won't believe it!' Marc, who is younger and less experienced, became panic-stricken. 'We must inform the authorities immediately!' he whispered. 'On the contrary,' Iliescu cut him short, 'we're not saying a word to anyone. This *could* create complications.' "

"I wonder why," Mărgărit interjected.

Eftimie coughed several times, emptied his glass, and lowered his voice. "Because Iliescu suspected what it might be about from the beginning. He didn't say so in front of Valentin, but to Marc he confided the next day that, very probably, it was some sort of military secret: probably a new system of camouflage by means of . . . here he mentioned a technical term I didn't understand. In any case, Iliescu repeated, the authorities, their colleagues, and above all the newspapers must not find out about their discovery. Because it was, indeed, a discovery. They kept watch on the following three nights and confirmed that they were not mistaken. They *saw* the trucks disappearing. Once two, another time five, and the third night one. It was true, Iliescu admitted, that on the third night—the fourth actually of their vigil—they were so tired they went home early."

"And yet, it was found out," Mărgărit interrupted, "if you say that Iliescu and all of us Romanians in France are under suspicion!"

"A piece of bad luck!" Eftimie exclaimed. "About two weeks ago, one evening, at a bar in Briançon, a discussion got started about 'flying saucers,' what are called today 'unidentified flying objects,' or 'UFOs.' Marc said— probably he had drunk too much—he said that he had seen some similarly mysterious means of transportation . . . and on the National Highway! He quickly realized his indiscretion and didn't go into details. Nevertheless, he had made a blunder, and a reporter who had been in the bar published the information that a new type of 'flying saucer' had been sighted near Briançon, and in a few days everybody in the whole region was talking about it. Imagine, therefore . . ."

Mărgărit got up from his chair suddenly, and signaling the others to be quiet, he went to the door. The moment the bell rang, he opened the door slowly, with great caution. Then, turning toward the others, he announced: "It's Dr. Tăusan!"

"Pardon me, dear friend," the doctor apologized, entering. "I'm being followed! Probably you were followed here too," he said, addressing Eftimie. "We're all being followed! I came to warn you. If they ask us what we were discussing in the Excelsior, let's be sure we're in agreement, so we don't contradict one another."

"That is—?" interjected Eftimie. "In what sense?"

"So we all say the same thing: that Iliescu was discreet and didn't divulge any details; that he told us that as a result of a *malentendu,* an article appeared in a newspaper in Midi and that . . ."

Again Mărgărit put his finger to his lips and started toward the door, treading lightly. Dr. Tăusan sat down on the couch. After a few minutes, not hearing the doorbell, Mărgărit called out, "*Qui est là?*"

And because there was no answer, he repeated the question in a sterner voice: "*Qui est là?*"

"*Nous venons de la part de monsieur Iliescu.*"

"*Mais j'ai des invités,*" Mărgărit began. "*Quelques amis.*"

"*Monsieur Iliescu nous a prié de vous consulter.*"

Squaring his shoulders like a soldier, Mărgărit opened the door wide. When he saw them entering—a tall young man, thin and blond, accompanied by a robust well-dressed, older man with a jolly face—Dr. Tăusan leaned toward Eftimie and whispered, "They aren't the ones who were following me!"

With some solemnity, Mărgărit made the introductions: "Monsieur Jean Boissier"—and the young man bowed his head politely—"and Monsieur Gerald Lascaze." Then he brought two more chairs from the dining room.

"*Mais de quoi s'agit-it?*" asked Tăusan.

"Let's speak Romanian," Inspector Lascaze began, smiling very cordially, "because I don't have very many chances to, and I like the Romanian language very much."

"If I didn't detect a very slight accent," exclaimed Eftimie, "I'd swear you were a Romanian yourself!"

Lascaze looked at his companion, amused, and laughed in a surprisingly spontaneous and friendly way.

"I spent my childhood in Romania, and my wife's Romanian. I'm sorry to disturb you," he continued, addressing the doctor and Eftimie, "but, as you've guessed, things are getting complicated. That's why the engineer Iliescu suggested we consult you. We know what you discussed last Sunday at the Excelsior, and this compounds the confusion."

"But why?" asked Eftimie and Tăusan together.

Lascaze laughed again, much amused, turning his head toward Boissier.

"Because you weren't alone in the cafe. There were others present who knew Romanian. And we're in danger of the story about what happened at Briançon being repeated—the article from *La Dépêche* about the UFO, and so forth."

"But Iliescu says that the flying saucers and all the rest are nonsense!" Eftimie exclaimed.

"This is precisely what's so serious," continued Lascaze in a somewhat official tone. "Domnul Iliescu has told you that according to his impression, it must have to do with a military secret, and this is more serious than unidentified flying objects. That's why we had to resort to certain precautionary measures. You found out, certainly, that traffic was prohibited in the area for twenty-four hours and since then has been rigorously supervised. We can speak about this . . . it's no secret. I'm informing you confidentially that we probably will be forced to invite—oh, just for a few days!—invite all of you to a hotel on Corsica: everyone, that is, who found out directly or through a third party about Valentin Iconeru's statement that he saw his former professor of history in an automobile, and that he even spoke with him."

"But that Valentin is an imbecile!" Eftimie interjected, starting to rise from the armchair. "How can you give any credence to what a young fellow says who barely speaks French?!"

Smiling ironically, Lascaze exchanged looks with his associate again.

"*Mais Valentin parle assez bien le française,*" said Boissier, "*et il est très apprécié au Musée. Il a fait des observations sensationellez sur les coléoptères de la zone alpine. On lui a publié plusiers articles. Bien entendu, sous un pseudonyme,*" he added with meaning, casting his eyes in Lascaze's direction.

"*En tout cas, . . .*" began Dr. Tăusan.

"Let's continue in Romanian," Lascaze broke in. "I feel more 'at home' in it, if you'll pardon the expression."

"In any case," Tăusan began again, "it seems to me *insulting,* if you'll excuse the expression, or at least exaggerated, to be suspected and possibly invited to Corsica just because Valentin claims that he's seen his former history teacher who supposedly said . . ."

" 'When we shall meet,'" Lascaze broke in, " 'in the shadow of a lily in Paradise.' "

Postăvaru flushed and reached for his handkerchief. He didn't dare lift his eyes to look at Mărgărit.

"In other words, you know about that too," whispered Eftimie. "You know about Liceul Sfântul Sava."

"Domnul Iliescu told us," explained Lascaze.

"It all started there," Eftimie continued, "with their professor. What purpose did he have in speaking to them, mere lycée boys, about the shadow of lilies in Paradise?"

"I've wondered the same thing myself," Lascaze interjected. "But, for the time being, it isn't *this* problem that interests me."

He glanced at his watch, and continued.

"I'd like for us to dwell a little on this phrase. My associate, who reads and understands Romanian but doesn't speak it, wishes me to ask you if this expression, 'in the shadow of a lily,' doesn't have for you Romanians some special meaning, if it isn't perhaps a metaphor."

"A metaphor?" repeated the doctor. "You mean, that it refers to something else in Romanian? But what?"

Lascaze gave him a long, scrutinizing look, then cast his eyes around the room at the others.

"For instance, the return from Exile," he suggested finally. "Because Jean Boissier has had many talks with Valentin (his secret passion is etymology), and in their talks he has gotten the impression that for Valentin, the Exile means more than the condition of being a refugee, as we understand it. He was struck, once, by something Valentin said: that the 'whole world lives in Exile, but only a few know it.' "

"*Une infime minorité,*" Boissier specified.

"And my associate wonders if the meeting in the shadow of a lily in Paradise might not refer to a blissful, triumphant return from Exile, as the Israelites returned from the Babylonian Captivity. Obviously," he added after a pause, "in this case it would not be a matter of East European exiles only, but of the great majority of Europeans."

"I'd never thought of such a thing," confessed the doctor.

"Nor I," Eftimie avowed.

Lascaze waited a few moments before resuming.

"You know what Valentin answers every time domnul Iliescu asks him to tell him in what circumstances he met his former history professor and spoke with him. He replies that he doesn't dare say, because no one would take him seriously!"

"But how can a man of science like Iliescu . . ." Dr. Tăusan began.

"That's another problem," Lascaze interrupted, "and it's an even more serious one. Iliescu met Valentin the last time exactly one week ago, after Valentin telephoned him from the Museum. In parentheses, be it said that when he disappears, he never informs Iliescu where he goes. Iliescu found out, through that telephone call a week ago, that Valentin had been coming to Paris to work at the Museum. Well, when we met him then, Valentin answered, perhaps jokingly, that he would consent to tell everything that has happened to either a leading religious personality or a great scientific figure."

"What impertinence!" Eftimie exclaimed.

Lascaze looked at him and smiled.

"This, obviously, has put us in a bind," he continued. "We consulted with the necessary persons, and we found a major religious personality whom Valentin will trust. But we wasted several days' time. When we informed domnul Iliescu of the news, we both took a plane to Briançon to bring Valentin back (he stayed in Paris only two days), but he had disappeared. That is, we haven't found him yet."

"Although," Dr. Tăusan intervened, smiling, "I imagine he too was being followed."

"Naturally he was being followed, as was d-l Iliescu, from the moment the article appeared in *La Dépêche*, and as you gentlemen have been, and still are."

"We know," murmured Eftimie.

"And yet," said Mărgărit, "it's impossible for you not to find him. An individual, a young foreigner, can't stay hidden very long."

"Of course we'll locate him," Lascaze agreed. "But we're losing valuable time. Already we've lost a great deal. I don't suppose that any of you gentlemen has run into this Valentin in the past few days?"

"No!" Eftimie declared emphatically, and the others shook their heads vigorously.

When the telephone rang, Boissier glanced at his watch and, standing up suddenly, he said to Mărgărit, "*Je m'excuse. C'est pour nous!*"

He lifted the receiver and listened for several moments without saying a word. Then he looked at Lascaze and shook his head. Lascaze drew up his chair, sat down, and took the receiver. At first he didn't attempt to hide his surprise, but as the conversation continued, his face became increasingly bright.

"*Perfect!*" he exclaimed at length, and gave Boissier a meaningful look. As he continued to listen, he consulted his watch from time to time. Finally he said softly, "*Tant mieux!*" and replaced the receiver quietly in its cradle. For a few moments he hesitated as though trying to decide what to do next. He looked about the room, fixing his gaze in turn on each of the four, who appeared somewhat cowed. Then he drew the chair close to the couch and sat down again.

"*Et alors?*" asked Dr. Tăusan.

"The latest news is good, but at the same time things are more complicated. What I can tell you is that Valentin was received in an audience with His Eminence, the Archbishop of Paris. How Valentin knew that an audience had been set for today at 3:00 o'clock, and that it was with the Archbishop, we will find out later. For the time being, His Eminence has telephoned the responsible persons and has related the contents of his interview with Valentin. I can't go into detail, but I believe that I commit no indiscretion in saying that His Eminence was very impressed by the— shall we say—'revelations' of the young naturalist. Moreover," he added, smiling, "Valentin will spend the night tonight at the Archiepiscopacy, and His Eminence has asked permission for Valentin to accompany him tomorrow when he flies to Rome."

"*Alors, le vieux a compris!*" murmured Boissier.

"*Hélas, les autres aussi!*" Lascaze replied between his teeth. "*Le pauvre pilote!* It seems that the audience with the Holy Father was arranged long ago," he added, turning to the others.

"But what did Valentin say?" the doctor boldly interrupted. "What sort of 'revelations' did he communicate?"

Lascaze shrugged, no longer trying to smile. "I hope I'll find out myself later on. His Eminence assured us, however, that the expression 'in the shadow of a lily in Paradise,' doesn't contain any heretical element. He invited us to read Gospels and the Church Fathers."

"But what about the ex-professor of history whom Valentin is supposed to have met?" Eftimie spoke up.

"His Eminence didn't say exactly, but he stated only that he has no reason to doubt his reality."

"So he's alive!" Mărgărit exclaimed. "But where? In what country?"

"This we shall find out later also. For the present, what interests us—both us and you Romanians in France—is the fact that you will no longer be obliged to spend the next five or six days at a hotel in Corsica."

"Finally, a piece of goods news!" exclaimed the doctor.

"Very good news, from all points of view," Lascaze agreed.

Eftimie shifted his position noisily in the armchair, preparing to speak.

"But what about the trucks?" Mărgărit inquired suddenly.

"Just what I was going to ask," Eftimie broke in. "Really, those trucks that disappear—do they or don't they *exist?*" And seeing that Lascaze had turned his eyes toward Boissier, he continued: "Or, as Iliescu believes, is it a matter of a military secret?"

"That's why I said the news was good, but at the same time it complicates things," Lascaze began. "It complicates things because we won't be able to observe them anymore. From now on, the enigma of the motor vehicles which become invisible at a precise point in space and a given moment in time will be the concern of others."

"What do you mean?" asked Eftimie.

"Valentin assured His Eminence that these mysterious trucks have changed their itinerary. From now on, their route will pass through a neutral country."

"*Un pays neutre?*" Boissier asked, frowning.

Lacaze turned and gazed at him long and calmly. "*C'est ce qu'il a dit, et il l'a répété: un pays neutre.*"

Boissier jumped up from his chair. "*Mais, il s'agit d'une métaphore!*" he exclaimed. "*Je connais bien Valentin; it nous faut le rejoindre. Et assez vite!*"

Lascaze stood up too, somewhat troubled. Then the telephone rang again, and, after hesitating a moment, Mărgărit picked up the receiver.

"Who? Ah, yes. Right. He's here. I'll put him on."

He motioned to Eftimie. "It's domnul Iliescu. He wants to speak with you."

Everyone stood up and waited anxiously. Eftimie listened with a rather solemn expression, shaking his head as usual. From time to time he shrugged his shoulders, irritated, but he did not venture to utter a word. Only after some minutes did he speak, and then in a whisper.

"Yes, they're here too.... I'll tell them. In fact, several men are here. I'll tell them all.... Good!"

He turned around looking triumphant, yet pensive. He started back to his chair, then stopped, changed his mind, and remained standing like all the others.

"It was Iliescu," he began. "Valentin called him by phone fifteen minutes ago, told him where we were, and asked him to give us a message for him. But I'll be damned if I understood what Valentin meant by his message! I understood only that *for the time being* we are in no danger. But we must not forget that the Exile is nearing its end, and we must prepare for the end of it *now*. 'How shall we prepare?' Iliescu asked him. 'That depends on the individual,' Valentin replied. And he went on: 'The one who has never loved flowers must learn to love them. Only thus will he understand the secret that children know, but which they soon forget.' And Iliescu told me something else," Eftimie added, embarrassed, "but I didn't understand, and I've forgotten it already."

"Something about the shadow of the lilies in Paradise?" suggested Postăvaru.

"No!" replied Eftimie sharply. "About *that* I'd have remembered. But, please, don't interrupt, because I'm afraid I'll get Valentin's recommendations mixed up. So, after the matter of the flowers, Valentin said: 'The one who has never spoken to any animal but his cat or dog should try to talk with other animals too—for instance, with birds in parks, or snakes in the *Jardin des Plantes*. He mustn't be discouraged if at first he doesn't understand their replies. With love and patience he *will* understand them—and then he'll begin to wake up and marvel at the splendor of his own existence,' or something like that. I can't remember his exact expression. And he told me something else," Eftimie added after a short pause, "but I didn't understand. 'For example'—and Iliescu repeated this sentence twice—'for example, we should look at the sky *without* stars and at empty train coaches with the lights turned out, we should smile *especially* at the old men and old women we meet on the street...' and other things I didn't understand and haven't retained."

"But what about Iliescu?" Dr. Tăusan interjected. "What was Iliescu's reaction?"

Eftimie hesitated and laid his hands on the back of the armchair as if he wanted to rest them.

"Iliescu seemed very much impressed," he continued, fixing his gaze momentarily on Lascaze's face. "He said: 'Valentin was right, not I. He understood.'"

"*What* did he understand?" Mărgărit insisted.

"That's all he said: that *Valentin understood*."

"But what about the trucks that disappear after midnight?" Tăusan asked.

Eftimie removed his hands from the chair back, took out his handkerchief, and wiped his forehead.

"Iliescu made only an allusion to them. But he told me that all Valentin had said to him on the phone—the message he asked him to transmit to us—all these things have allowed him—and will allow us—to understand why only *certain* trucks disappear and what happens to them. Then we shall understand also what awaits us, that is, what will happen to *some* of us."

"So far, I don't understand any of this!" Lascaze exclaimed, starting for the door. But stopping abruptly, he addressed Eftimie: "Where did Iliescu call from?"

"From a telephone booth. He said there were two or three people waiting in line, and that was why he was in such a hurry."

"And we're in a hurry too!" said Lascaze, shaking hands with Eftimie.

At the door, he turned his head toward Boissier who had taken out his pocket appointment book and was leafing through it perplexedly.

"*Il faut nous presser, mon vieux!*"

"But he said something else," Eftimie murmured. "He said he was leaving this very evening."

Lascaze began to laugh. "It doesn't matter. We'll be going with him. And he won't be surprised when he sees us. The engineer Iliescu has known for a long time that he was being followed step by step."

Eftimie shook his head, then added timidly: "I didn't want to repeat what he said just before he hung up."

Lascaze looked at him quizzically. "What did he say?"

"He said for you not to bother following him anymore—that he has done his duty and has conveyed the message to you."

"That's what *he* thinks!" Lascaze rejoined. "But there are other problems we have to discuss."

Eftimie wiped his hands, one after the other, with his handkerchief.

"He also said, 'If Inspector Lascaze insists, at all costs, on meeting me, ask him to wait for me tomorrow morning, between 2:00 and 3:00, at kilometer 109 on the Băle-Schaffhausen Highway. But we won't be able to talk. I'll be in the third truck, along with Valentin's former history professor.' "

"*Sans blague?*" exclaimed Lascaze, much amused. "And did he not say something else?"

"He said, 'Thank Inspector Gerald Lascaze for being so amiable, and remind him of our first discussion. If, that evening, when we were separating—if he hadn't said to me, "*Heureux les pacifiques,*" who knows what would have become of my soul?' "

They could hear the two men hurrying down the stairs, because the host had remained standing in the doorway, holding open the door. When they were gone, Mărgărit dropped exhausted into a chair.

Eftimie spoke in a very weak voice: "I don't know if I did the right thing or not, not to tell them everything."

Mărgărit turned his head in surprise.

"I repeated only Valentin's message," continued Eftimie. "But I didn't tell them the conclusion Iliescu has reached regarding the trucks that disappear. Iliescu said: 'Valentin was right. A new Noah's Ark is being made ready.' "

"In what sense?" Mărgărit inquired, much troubled.

"Those mysterious vehicles are transporting many people selected from all countries. The trucks don't vanish, but they pass into a space with other dimensions than those of our space."

"Speak more clearly, man!" Mărgărit demanded, interrupting again.

Eftimie smiled melancholically. "I don't understand very well myself what happens, but Iliescu told me that actually it's a matter of a camouflage, serving the same functions as any other camouflage: that is, to hide, but at the same time to attract the attention of those who have been informed in advance. Iliescu specified—and this I can repeat verbatim—that 'the passage to the new Noah's Ark can be effected instantaneously and in an invisible way, but, for our own good, it is sometimes camouflaged by means of a truck.' "

"Why, *for our own good?*" the doctor inquired.

"He didn't have time to explain that to me. But from all he did say, I understand that it has to do with certain signs that are made to us, and which some of us discern. Because, he repeated: 'Dear Eftimie, signs of all sorts are being made to us continually. Open your eyes and try your best to decipher them!' "

"That means," Mărgărit exclaimed sadly, "that the end of the world is near. The Flood! The Apocalypse!"

"No, no!" Eftimie interrupted. "Iliescu assured me that signs have been made to us for a long time, for centuries. Only the camouflage changes—according to the age in which we live. Today, in our era dominated by technology . . ."

Mărgărit stood up suddenly and placed himself directly in front of Eftimie, staring at him quizzically. "But Iliescu didn't tell you *that*—the matter about this being an era dominated by technology."

Eftimie blushed, smiling sheepishly. "No, he didn't actually say that. He didn't have time, anyway. But I guessed it myself, a little while ago. Really, Valentin and Iliescu are right. Signs *are* being made to us, but we pass them by without seeing them."

And because Mărgărit kept staring at him in disbelief, he continued.

"Take, for instance, our meeting today: four Romanians, two Frenchmen, and two telephone calls; and all of these—the meeting, the conversations, the calls—having something to do with the same expression: 'in the shadow of a lily in Paradise.' Doesn't that strike you as strange?"

For some moments the other three men stared at him, troubled and hesitant.

"So, in conclusion," the doctor said, venturing to break the silence, "what do you think will happen to us?"

Eftimie sat down calmly in the armchair.

"Let's wait a little while," he said with a smile. "Maybe the telephone will ring again, or the doorbell."

"Even if one of them were to ring," began Mărgărit, "even if . . ."

But he broke off his sentence and, turning pale, he hurried to the telephone and lifted the receiver.

"Hello! Hello!"

He waited a few moments, then repeated, almost shouting:

"Hello! Hello!"

The doctor approached, frowning at him.

"He doesn't answer," Mărgărit murmured.

After awhile he replaced the receiver and added, "No one's there!"

Chicago, April 1982, and Eygalières, August 1982

About the Contributors

Lawrence G. Desmond, whose photographs of the Eliades appear in this volume, was primarily responsible for the photographic collection of the Mesoamerican Archive and Research Project at the University of Colorado. He received his M.A. from the Universidad de las Americas in Mexico and his Ph.D. in anthropology from the University of Colorado. His publications include *A Dream of Maya: Augustus and Alice Le Plongeon in Nineteenth-Century Yucatan* (1988).

Joseph M. Kitagawa, friend and colleague of Mircea Eliade, was formerly dean of the Divinity School at the University of Chicago. He has published numerous articles and books on the history of religions. His most recent publications include *On Understanding Japanese Religion* (1987) and *The Quest for Human Unity: A Religious History* (1990).

Edward P. Nolan, professor of English and comparative literature at the University of Colorado, Boulder, received his B.A. from Yale and his Ph.D. in comparative literature from Indiana University in 1966. His published works include *American Literary Manuscripts: A Checklist of Holdings in Academic, Historical and Public Libraries, Museums and Authors' Homes in the United States* (1978) and *Now Through a Glass Darkly: Specular Images of Being and Knowing from Virgil to Chaucer* (1991).

Robert A. Pois, professor of history at the University of Colorado, Boulder, received his Ph.D. in 1965 from the University of Wisconsin. His published works include *Emile Nolde* (1982), *The Bourgeois Democrats of Weimar Germany* (1976); *Friedrich Meinecke and German Politics in the 20th Century* (1972); *Alfred Rosenberg: Selected Writings* (1970) published in the United States as *Race and Race History and Other Essays;* and *National Socialism and the Religion of Nature* (1986).

Mac Linscott Ricketts is professor and chair of the Department of Religion and Philosophy at Louisburg College, North Carolina. From 1959 to 1964, he studied with Mircea Eliade at the University of Chicago. He has translated several of Eliade's literary works including *Youth Without Youth and Other Stories* (1989) and is currently translating into Romanian *Mircea Eliade: The Romanian Roots, 1907–1945.*

Rodney L. Taylor, professor of religious studies and associate dean of the graduate school at the University of Colorado, Boulder, received his Ph.D. in Chinese religion from Columbia University. Among his published works are *The Cultivation of Sagehood as a Religious Goal in New-Confucianism* (1978); *The Way of Heaven: An Introduction to the Confucian Life* (1986); *The Confucian Way of Contemplation: Okada Takehiko and the Tradition of Quiet Sitting* (1988); and *They Shall Not Hurt: Human Suffering and Human Caring* (1989).

About the Book and Editors

This book creates a visual and literary record that reflects the deliberations of a year-long seminar of scholars on the literary, autobiographical, and academic works of the brilliant humanist and historian of religions, Mircea Eliade. This tribute combines excellent photographs of Professor Eliade, selections from all three genres of his writings, and short essays by scholars who worked with Professor Eliade in a seminar in Boulder, Colorado. The unifying thread of the book — best expressed by Eliade in his 1982 lecture "Waiting for the Dawn" — is Eliade's vision of literary creativity and the academic study of religion as a basis for a New Humanism.

David Carrasco received his Ph.D. in history of religions from the University of Chicago in 1977. His publications include *Quetzalcoatl and the Irony of Empire: Myths and Prophecies in the Aztec Tradition* and *To Change Place: Aztec Ceremonial Landscapes*. He is currently professor of history of religions and director of the Mesoamerican Archive and Research Project at the University of Colorado, Boulder.

Jane Marie Law received her Ph.D. in 1990 from the Divinity School at the University of Chicago. The title of her dissertation is "Puppets of the Road: Ritual Performance in Japanese Folk Religion." She is currently asistant professor of Asian Studies at Cornell University.

Mircea Eliade